"If you're interested in assuring that you obt
your spells and are willing to put the work in.
the book for you. Completely filled with some amazing insights, ideas,
and tips that come from experience. [Miller's] ideas are some that I've
never seen in other books. This book alone completely changed how I
approach giving offerings to spirits and deities."

—**Mat Auryn**, author of *Psychic Witch*

"If you are searching for a sagacious instructor of magick, look no further.
In this new edition of the modern must-have, Jason Miller embodies the
wise teacher who blends his vast knowledge of the esoteric with excellent
structure, infused with his wry humor. You'll feel personally guided by a
masterful sorcerer who's taken the considerable time to review and update
his teachings, thus providing the reader with both the foundational
lessons and a deeper understanding. Highly informative and enjoyable."

—**Cyndi Brannen**, author of *Entering Hekate's Cave*, *Entering Hekate's Garden*, and *Keeping Her Keys*

"Jason's teachings are mandatory for new occultists who want to
understand tradition, but also practice methods. This book is a great mix
of education and also step-by-step ways to start bringing powerful magic
into your modern life."

—**Chaweon Koo**, author of *Spell Bound: A New Witch's Guide to Crafting the Future*

"When I met Jason Miller, the first edition of this book had just come
out, but I was not yet familiar with his work. However, right away, I
knew that I'd met a Real Sorcerer. Unlike so many people I'd met in the
magical community, he was neither wicked nor weak, neither pretentious
nor simple. After speaking with him, I was eager to learn more about
the sort of magic he practiced. I learned a lot from *The Sorcerer's Secrets*,
and I've recommended it to many others, both beginners to magic and
those who want to reinvigorate a stale practice. This new edition, with its
additional context and commentary, brings a mature wisdom and twenty-
first century outlook to what was already an outstanding book. It is a true
classic. I am delighted to be able to recommend *Real Sorcery* to a new
generation of magicians."

—**Sara Mastros**, author of *The Sorcery of Solomon*

Real Sorcery

Strategies for
Powerful Magick

STRATEGIC SORCERY SERIES

JASON MILLER

WEISER BOOKS

ALSO BY JASON MILLER

Consorting with Spirits

The Elements of Spellcrafting

Financial Sorcery

Protection and Reversal Magick

Sex, Sorcery, and Spirit

This edition first published in 2023 by Weiser Books, an imprint of
Red Wheel/Weiser, LLC

With offices at:
65 Parker Street, Suite 7
Newburyport, MA 01950
www.redwheelweiser.com
www.newpagebooks.com

ISBN: 978-1-57863-800-0

Library of Congress Control Number: 2023930508

Cover design by Sky Peck Design
Cover art by Wojciech Zwoliński/Cambion Art
Interior photos/images by Matthew Brownlee
Interior by Debby Dutton
Typeset in Adobe Garamond, Frutiger LT, and Warnock

Printed in the United States of America
IBI

10 9 8 7 6 5 4 3 2 1

This work is dedicated to the memory of
James W. Flemming, 1974–2008.

CONTENTS

Part Two: Strategic Sorcery 63

ACKNOWLEDGMENTS

First and foremost, I wish to thank my wife for her patience and encouragement during the writing of this book. Thanks also to my mother and father for raising me in an environment that was conducive to learning the magickal arts, and for always encouraging me in my esoteric pursuits, no matter how strange they seemed or how far away they took me.

Special thanks to Matthew Brownlee for more than twenty years of friendship and for providing all the artwork for this book. Bang up job, my friend.

Thanks also to: Frater Xanthias for linguistic assistance; Albus Eddie for information on NLP and Ericksonian Hypnosis; John Myrdhin Reynolds for Tibetan translations and other help; and Sister Persephone and Frater Rufus Opus for impromptu copyediting.

Thanks to all my initiators, mentors, teachers, friends, and informants who have revealed to me the secrets of their craft. Special thanks for this go to: John Myrdhin Reynolds, Namkhai Norbu, Lopon Tenzin Namdak, Kunzang Dorje Rinpoche, Cliff and Misha

Pollick, catherine yronwode, Tau Nemesius, Paul Hume, Simon, Lama Wangdor, Blanch Krubner, Dr. Jim, and Susan Carbury.

My heartfelt gratitude to everyone that attended my monthly classes at Mystical Tymes in New Hope, Pennsylvania; The Cauldron in Point Pleasant, New Jersey; and The Full Moon in Mount Holly, New Jersey. Those classes and your feedback were instrumental in helping me evolve the ideas presented in this book. Thanks also to my fellow bloggers Frater R. O., Witchdoctor Joe, Frater B. H., "My Gal," Jack Faust, Mike Rock, and Sister Persephone.

Much appreciation to all the members of Thelesis Lodge, the Chthonic Auranian Temple, the Terra Sancta Sodality, the Wild Hunt Club, and the Ngakpa Zhonnu Khang Sangha for their continued fraternity and support.

Lastly, I want to thank everyone at Weiser Books who worked on this book. Specifically, Laurie Kelly-Pye who read an article of mine and suggested I start writing books, and her husband Michael Pye, who was extremely generous with deadline extensions for the present work.

INTRODUCTION

I am a professional Sorcerer. I not only write and teach the methods of magick, but I perform practical magick for clients that are seeking to change their lives for the better. Some students and clients are beginners or just regular people in need of a little magickal assistance, but many are actually longtime practitioners who just haven't been able to make the magick work for them. Often they have dozens of books on the subject and know many spells and rituals, but they haven't been able to get the results they hoped for. Perhaps they draw spiritual benefit from their path, but they haven't been able to make magick manifest materially in ways that they had expected.

They find themselves having invested a lot of time and effort into an art that they can't seem to make work for them. They may have even built their social lives around Witchcraft and the occult. Because they haven't been able to do magick successfully, they may have shifted their focus from the Sorcery that originally got them interested to either Pagan religious observance or psychological self-help. Both of these are good things. Magick *should* be used for spiritual evolution and mystical insight; but I am here to tell you that practical magick *does* work. Real results are possible; you just need to know how to go about it. Real change in the real world.

Of course, there are a lot of books that say that. Oodles of magickal books fill the shelves of nearly every bookstore in the world, making all kinds of promises of power and wisdom. How is this one different?

Recently, I took stock of what was available out there and noticed that books on magick generally fell into two categories: training manuals, or spell books.

The training manuals are mostly about learning the rituals and beliefs of a particular magickal order or type of Witchcraft. Much of the information relates only to the magick of spiritual development or worship, which are important, but are by no means the entirety of the art. Material that does relate to practical magick, when it's there at all, is often treated as a side issue.

On the other side of the spectrum, there are spell books. Spell books are great. I own lots of them, but they go only so far. You can pick one up and do a spell for something, but without the power and awareness to implement it skillfully, your spell has only a slim chance of achieving the desired result. Even if your spell works, do you know how to manage the result and build upon it? There is more to success in Sorcery than simply performing a ritual that you found in a book.

This book is neither a training manual nor a spell book. It is a *field manual.*

Voodoo Priest Louis Martinié once shared with me the following magickal axiom: *first comes the working, then comes the work.* There is a lot more to making successful magick than just the magick itself:

How do you attack a problem from multiple sides using magick?

How do you blend magickal and mundane action to
    achieve success?
How do you know whether what you are doing is working?
How do you fix it if it's not?
What are the best ways to work on behalf of others?

To answer these questions, I will present the usual exercises and
spells that you would find in a book of this sort, but, more than this,
I will present complete strategies for generating successful results. In
so doing I will be revealing many tips of the trade that even today are
often shared only within closed cabals or from mentor to student.

It is my hope that this book will aid in rescuing the art of magick
from those who have ignored, downplayed, or outright denied the
existence of practical Sorcery in favor of arcane titles, intangible
results, and fantasy attainments.

To those who think that spells are only psychological exercises
designed to build confidence or release stress; to those who think
Witchcraft is only religion and not a craft; to those who have come
to think that magick can affect only the mind of the magician and
not the minds of others; to those who have tried and failed, and have
given up on effecting the fabric of perception and probability; this
book intends to prove you wrong.

Jason Miller
Hallowmas, 2008

INTRODUCTION TO
THE NEW EDITION

This book was originally published under the title *The Sorcerer's Secrets*. It sounds like a title chosen by a publishing company, doesn't it? It totally was. I don't know how many secrets there are in the book, but as titles go, it was fine. Truth be told, *Real Sorcery* was chosen by Weiser as well, but it's a much better title that speaks to what this book is about.

Sorcery is real.

I think this is worth taking a moment to reflect upon because I talk to people every week that practice magick, Sorcery, and Witchcraft, but don't seem to grasp the full implications of it being real.

Sorcery is real, and as a real thing its influence competes against the influence of other real things. You can be sure that your love spell is hard at work, but so are your physical appearance, social skills, sense of humor, confidence, agreeability, and a dozen other factors. What this book asks is: are these factors working together to get you what you want, or are they working against each other?

Let's pick a number at random . . . say eight. Your love spell has an influence of eight. How would you rate the influence of these other factors? Maybe your face is a seven. That's good. Unfortunately, your hygiene is a negative four. Your confidence is a five, but your narcissistic tendency to make every conversation about yourself is a negative eight.

Sorcery is real and thus competes in the world with other real things.

If those real influences are working against you, your spell is fighting an uphill battle. Some people put so much effort into their Sorcery that they put nearly no effort into any other aspect of getting what they want. You can live in such a way that the most powerful and perfectly executed magick is needed just to get you to the baseline that you could have started at.

Sorcery is real, and as a real thing it can succeed or fail for entirely mechanical reasons. Magick failing to achieve a goal is different from magick not working. Doctors treat patients with effective medicine all the time and don't get the outcome that they hope for. It doesn't mean that the medicine didn't work, it just wasn't up to the task it was put up against. Same with lawyers, salespeople, and Olympic athletes. Our efforts must be up to the task. Yet, when a ritual or a spell fails, I rarely see people treat this as a normal part of practice.

When a spell or ritual doesn't get the effect we hope it should, some will point their fingers and take this as proof that magick isn't real, but that's not at all the case. My car jack can't lift the Empire State Building, but that doesn't make it not real.

Others will resort to extreme explanations to avoid admitting failure at all:

"The Gods did not will it to be so." If we can only do what God or Gods want, what's the point of magick at all?

"Your higher self protected you from yourself." Really? Where the hell was my higher self when I put money into FTX or dated that psycho in college?

"Your magick will manifest in due time. . . ." Thanks, magick, but the mortgage is due on the first of the month.

My favorite of these has to be: "Your magick manifested . . . on the astral plane. . . ." *Ugh.*

When we let go of both reflexive denials and woo-woo excuses, and look at Sorcery as a real thing, we can start to see the truth of the situation: what we did simply wasn't up to the task. We can then look for ways to do it better, find other approaches, or just walk away. In short, we examine and respond to what happened as if magick were any other real thing. Because it is.

Sorcery is real, and mastering real things takes a lot of time and effort. Rarely, some people are heavily gifted. Even more rarely, someone finds that they have no talent for it at all. Most of us, though, have a reasonable capability for it that can grow and strengthen the more we study and practice. As we progress, we find that within the overall art, we have strengths that can be affirmed and shortcomings that can be either overcome or circumvented. In short, it's just like anything else. I am not a naturally talented musician, and my fingers are short, but I can still whip out a mean version of "Me and the Devil" by Robert Johnson when I want to.

Yet, so many students throw in the towel if things don't come instantly and easily. They close their eyes to meditate and give up at the first distraction, forgetting that recognizing and releasing yourself from distraction is what meditation is about at the start. They say the words to an evocation, then rage quit if spirit doesn't instantly appear in the crystal, forgetting that it can take significant effort on both sides to make a bridge between worlds.

If magick is a fantasy for you, then of course you want it all to just jump to life because of how magickal you are, but if we accept that Sorcery is *real*, with everything that implies, then that expectation should dissipate like fairy dust, revealing the truth that it takes work to get good at things, and that discipline and persistence will outperform natural talent at every turn.

Sorcery is real, so you don't need a separate "magickal ethics." Magick, as a real thing, can be used for good or for ill or for anything in between. Most everything in the real world is in between, and the real world is where Sorcery operates. There is no need for "magickal ethics." The ethics you use to navigate the rest of life will do just fine. If you would use physical violence against someone, then using a curse is probably on the table. If you wouldn't ever consider hitting someone to get what you want, then cursing them should be off the table as well.

Most situations are not as cut and dried as curses, of course, and platitudes about causing no harm simply do not fit the reality. If you do a spell to get the VP slot at your company, this doesn't affect just you. It affects the other people who were up for the job that won't get it and will therefore suffer. So, does this make magick unethical? I don't think so. Not any more than being conventionally attractive, going to an impressive school, having good connections, or any manner of privilege. If you do a spell that specifies that your magick not harm anyone, you might just be enchanting yourself out of that job rather than into it.

That said, you don't want to attain your ends by any means either. There are things you will do to get what you want, and things you won't do to get what you want. All real actions have consequences, intentional and unintentional. Nonaction also has consequences. No one gets out of this world with clean hands, but that doesn't mean we need to be sociopaths either.

The one thing different about magick is that you won't get charged with assault or abuse for curses and bindings, but this doesn't change the ethical considerations. If anything, it reveals who you really are. If the only reason you aren't a monster is your fear of getting caught, that doesn't make you ethical.

Sorcery is real and therefore offers no absolute safety or success.

I remember years ago talking to a friend, an elder really, who was very clearly suffering from a curse. Not only did they have all the constellation of symptoms you might expect, but there was a person with both motivation and ability that all but admitted to performing the curse. Yet, this friend believed that this was simply impossible.

"I banish daily. Nothing can get through."

Foreign Policy Advisor Dan Caldwell once said, "There is no such thing as absolute security; it's a matter of degree." This is how real things work. You get into a car with airbags, wear your seat belt, and drive defensively in order to protect yourself and your passengers while driving, but you still can wind up dead. You can become a black belt in jiujitsu and still get the shit beat out of you. You can have all the security of a fully fortified military installation and still get wiped off the face of the earth. Real things don't exist in absolutes, and Sorcery is a real thing.

No matter what you do, something can still "get you."

So does that mean we shouldn't bother with protection magic? Of course not! We just need to recognize that it's a matter of degree. We prevent what dangers we can, we mitigate the damage we can't prevent, and we recover and rebuild from what harm we survive.

Should we max out protection then? Also no. We need to recognize that, whether they are spirits or people, most beings are not out to get us. Most beings don't really care about us one way or another. All security comes with a price. Endless banishings can cut you off from the very spirits that you should be contacting and learning from.

When we let go of the fantasy that Sorcery can keep us perfectly and absolutely safe or the delusion that spirits will take any opportunity to hurt us, we can start to evaluate our security needs and the methods we take to establish it. This is how real things work, and Sorcery is Real.

Sorcery is real and *Real Sorcery* is fit for the real world. I didn't write it just to show that magick was real though. I wrote it so that you could do magick that *matters*.

I have been doing magick since I was fifteen years old. I knew right away magick worked. In my twenties and early thirties, my life was pretty much held together by spells. Spells to pay the rent that month. Spells not to get laid off. Spells to find a girlfriend. Spells to keep her. Spells to finance months of travel to Europe and Asia. Spells to make ends meet when I got back home.

Sure, I did plenty of workings to gain illumination or wisdom too, but when it came to the material world, I seemed to always be fixing a problem, preventing a problem, or enchanting for short term gains.

The magick worked too. Sometimes spectacularly, even miraculously, well. I was not short on stories of paranormal occurrences or successful rituals. What I was short on was a meaningful and fulfilling life. In my mid-thirties, I came to a realization: The issue was not whether magick worked or not. The issue was what I was working it *for.*

You can have the best tool in the world, but if you use it on things that don't matter, it's not going to make much of a difference.

Aleister Crowley gave us our most popular definition of magick: "The art of causing change in accordance with will." I came to realize that "influence" is a more accurate word than "causing." If you want my definition, or at least my description of what it does, it is this: ***Magick is an influence on probability and minds.***

The distinction between influence and cause is important, especially when it comes to practical Sorcery and aiming it at things that will make a big difference in our lives. If we want to do magick that matters, we need to be skilled not only at the Sorcery, but also at the thing we are trying to enchant. This basic concept, which I call Strategic Sorcery, is the cornerstone of this book and remains the root of all my other teachings.

So now I have to expand this book, originally written in 2009. The question before me is: What can I tell you now, that I didn't tell you then, that will help you do Real Sorcery that matters?

Included in this book is a new section at the end of each chapter to update my thoughts on those individual topics, but here in this introduction I want to leave you a single piece of advice that I have found makes a huge difference. If you follow this simple rule, not only will the success rate of your spells skyrocket, but you will almost certainly be going after things that will make a big difference in your life. Here it is: **Make a plan that could work without magick, then use magick to make that plan work better.**

This is the cardinal rule of Strategic Sorcery. Think about it for a minute. If magick is an influence on minds and events, then don't you want as many influences going your way as possible? It just makes sense right? Figure out what you want, make a plan to achieve that thing that *might* work on its own, and then do magick to give that plan more mojo. This way your Sorcery is working hard at overcoming obstacles to your solid plan, rather than fighting an uphill battle to get you to the level that ordinary people are already operating from.

This does disrupt the fantasy, doesn't it? The fantasy is that some lonely soul without a pot to piss in summons a demon and is soon fending off underwear models while counting the piles of money that roll in from nowhere. There are still actually a lot of people who think that is how magick works, if only they follow the right formula to the letter. This is *not* how it works. If it were, Witchcraft conventions would be held at exclusive resorts in the Maldives every year instead of at the Holiday Inn in Wilmington.

"But Jason, what about miracles? What about truly paranormal results? Don't they happen?"

They do. I have witnessed many. Most people who practice magick or Witchcraft have. They happen, but they don't happen regularly. You can't count on them happening repeatedly. Celebrate the miracles, unexplainable phenomena, and jaw dropping strangenesses when they happen. They will happen for sure. But if you want to be a Sorcerer, Sorceress, or Sorcerix whose magick has a meaningful impact, my advice is not to live in such a way that you require the complete breaking of reality to claim success!

ABOUT THE MAGICK
IN THIS BOOK

Rather than use the more common terms *Witchcraft* or *magick,* I have chosen to refer to the magick in this book as *Sorcery.*

The term *Witch* tends to conjure the idea of a style of magick that values the feminine over the masculine, the intuition over the intellect, the lunar over the solar, the nocturnal over the daylight, the ecstatic over the ceremonial, the outdoors over the temple, the chthonic over the ouranic, and so on. It doesn't reject the latter in each case, it simply emphasizes the former. The term *magician,* on the other hand, tends to invoke the opposite juxtapositions.

I say that we must transcend the dichotomy, and thus encompass both ends of this spectrum! Thus, I have chosen the term Sorcerer, which, to me at least, contains elements of both the Witch and the magician.

Furthermore, the term *Sorcerer* is almost always used in connection with practical magick, the focus of this book. While the Witch might be concerned with the ecstasy of the Sabbat and worship of old gods, and the magician might spend all his time climbing the tree of life and exploring the astral, the Sorcerer is most definitely engineering change on the material plane.

This is not to say that the Sorcerer, Sorceress, or Sorcerix is not religious or mystical, only that the Sorcerer reflects his insights out into the world through action. *Thaumaturgy*, Greek for wonder working, is the outward expression of his *Theurgy*, or illuminative work.

To accomplish his work, the Sorcerer seamlessly employs methods both magickal and mundane. When seeking to build wealth, he pays as much attention to mastering the skills of money management and career building as he does to the summoning of spirits and use of spells. He doesn't care whether it is the mundane or the magickal work that finally leads him to success, only that success is attained.

I have made no effort to focus on one tradition at the exclusion of another. We no longer live in a purely traditional culture. Modern modes of communication and travel have made the world much smaller than it once was. The chance that a Santero or Peruvian Shaman will cross paths with a Jewish Kabbalist or British Witch is now a very real possibility. In fact, it happens all the time. Without going out of my way to seek anyone out specifically, I was exposed to a Rosicrucian teacher, a Rootworker, a Santera, a Buddhist Ngakpa, and several different Wiccans all within central New Jersey, and all before I was twenty years old! Thus, you will find spells that have their roots in African American Hoodoo, alongside of ones inspired by European folk magick and ones that stem from Himalayan Tantric Sorcery. Tech is tech after all, and what works is what works, be it magick or machinery. As Aleister Crowley said, "Success be thy proof." In order to pay respect to these traditions in their own cultural context, I encourage you to check the source material at the end of the book for further study.

The symbol shown on the next page was designed and rendered by my friend and fellow Sorcerer Matthew Brownlee to represent the style of magick that I am presenting in the book. It is a sort of heraldic crest for this teaching and deserves some explanation.

The hand with the eye at the center is an ancient and widespread symbol known by many names: the Hamsa, the Hand of Fatima, the Hand of Miriam, and the Zos Kia to name just a few. In this case, it represents the union of mystical insight (eye) and worldly action (hand). Above the hand are the sun and moon conjoined, representing the union and transcendence of opposites. On the wrist of the hand is the alchemical symbol for Prime, the base of all. The eye in the hand sheds a tear to represent both the trials of training and the presence of the Sangreal, or sacred blood. The key and torch crossed behind the hand represent again the union of insight and illumination (torch) and action (the key). The serpent that surrounds the hand has numerous meanings and can be thought of as the serpent of knowledge, a symbol of transformation, and of the inner power of the subtle body. Because it eats its tail, it is also a symbol of eternal return. The symbols in the serpent all relate to royal stars that have particular importance at the current time. They can be switched out for other stars as ye will, and indeed there are greater mysteries in this symbol that I will leave unspoken. Some things must be discovered in order to be meaningful.

Part One
Basic Training

CHAPTER 1

The Gift

Every endeavor in life has a base, a path, and a fruit. Magick is no different, and so we must start by examining our base, the point at which we start. Most books on magick suggest the base or starting point is the same for everyone, that we are all, more or less, equally talented, and that everyone can accomplish every task with enough effort. Books promising that "anyone can do it" are as common in the magick section of the store as they are on the self-help and home-repairs shelves. Sadly, this isn't necessarily the case.

We are an egalitarian society and like to think that we are all created equal. Although I agree that all life has equal inherent value, that doesn't mean that we are all equally gifted at all things. Just as some people are born with innate talent in music, mathematics, or art, some people are born with innate talent for magick. If you are not particularly gifted in something, you can usually make up for it with hard work and practice, but sadly, just as there are tone deaf people who would like to make music or numerically challenged people who would love to be scientists, there are also people with almost no gift for magick. Some of you won't like to hear that, but it's true.

In older days, only people who had some gift or calling would have even considered studying magick. In most cultures, even ones in which magick is recognized and accepted as real, a career in magick or spirituality is not something that someone would undertake unless they felt strongly pulled in that direction. In Haiti, the Loa have been known to coerce gifted people into becoming Houngans and Mambos by making them ill until they enter training. It is the same in Nepal with Jankris (Shamans). Certainly, the strong taboo against Sorcery in the Western world, with penalties ranging from ridicule to execution, has in the past been enough to weed out those who had only cursory interest. Only those with a burning need would even consider undertaking any type of occult study.

Today, however, the situation is a bit different. Magick is big business and Witchcraft is popular. Rather than attracting only those who have a gift for the work, the arts attract hundreds of people who have no real calling for, or sometimes even an interest in, practical magick. They might be interested in Paganism as a religion, or magick as a countercultural statement. Some join a coven or order simply because other people in their social circle are doing it. These folks may try out a spell or two, but if they don't get immediate results, they stop trying because the magick isn't really what drew them in in the first place. There is nothing wrong with spiritual development or religion, but if people who aren't interested in or who don't even believe in practical magick keep calling themselves Witches and magicians, it causes a bit of confusion. As Robert Cochrane once pointed out, the world is filled with Witches who cannot perform the tasks of Witchcraft. This is yet another reason why I choose the term *Sorcerer*.

Now, before you get the idea that only a few lucky souls who are born with a caul[1] or are the seventh son of a seventh son can be successful Sorcerers, let me ease your mind by telling you that effort

Real Sorcery

in developing your gift is far more important than your innate gift. Many people have powerful gifts, but put no effort into developing them, and thus produce shaky results, if any at all. Conversely, many people who have only modest gifts but put a lot of time into developing them turn out to be successful Sorcerers.

Besides innate gift and training, there is another element of the equation for successful Sorcery: *implementation*. You can have amazing gifts at magick, spending hours every day in meditation, study, and ritual, but still not know how to apply your talents in practical situations.

Imagine a man who wants to move a boulder. He is born with a large frame and good genes so he has the gift of strength. He trains in the gym and *develops* his muscles to the point where he is as strong as he can be. But when it comes time to move the boulder, if he doesn't know how to apply his strength, he still won't be able to move it. He needs to know about how to use a lever and where to place that lever for maximum effect. His natural strength is his *gift*. His weight training is his *development*. The lever and the knowledge of how to use it are *implementation*. Remember the following:

(Gift × Development) + Skillful Implementation = Success

So how do we know if we have a gift? There are some traditional signs we can look at that appear at birth. We already mentioned being born with a caul or being the seventh son of a seventh son as a couple examples. Being born on Halloween, having a stillborn twin, or simply not crying as a baby are other signs that people have pointed to through the centuries as marks of spiritual gifts.

There are also signs that can appear after important psychic events such as initiation or visitation by spirits. Witch hunters in the 16th and 17th centuries were obsessed with the idea that the Devil leaves a mark on his Witches after initiating them in midnight sabbats. The grisly practice of pricking Witches with needles, looking for Devil's marks or Witch's teats that felt no pain, was a major part of the inquisition's methods. There may have been a grain of truth to the legend, however. There are several lineages of traditional Witchcraft that acknowledge Cain as the progenitor of Witchblood and say that they possess a spiritual "mark of Cain" that can be seen by those who also possess the blood. There are Basque and Italian lineages of Witchcraft that take pride in Lucifer bestowing a similar mark.

Beliefs that gifts of magickal power come from bloodlines that have been mixed with angelic, fey, or demonic blood are actually fairly common. The Grigori or Watchers spoken of in Genesis 6 and in the Book of Enoch are said to have mated with human women and given birth to a race of giants and men renowned for their great powers. There are many English and Irish legends about changelings, people who possess "fey-touched" or "pixilated" blood, because they descend from humans that have been kidnapped and raped by fairies.

One of the magickal groups that I belong to is the Sangreal Sodality. As everyone that has read or seen *The Da Vinci Code* now knows, Sangreal means "Royal Blood." In our case, however, we are not talking about the bloodline of Christ as a historical person, but an angelic or divine strain in the bloodline. In fact the words *blest* and *blessed* come from old English *bloedsian*, meaning "to be consecrated by blood." Although this strain may have at some point been within only royal families, it is widespread now.[2] We believe that through training in magick, you can awaken this divine spark and bless yourself and others.

This idea of the gift of magick being passed by blood is part of the motive behind ancestor worship in most African Traditional Religions, and also the cause for celebrating saints and other spiritual masters from the past. By celebrating and invoking the lives of those who came before us in blood or in tradition, we make part of their experiences our own.

In the East, it is your former incarnations that are typically thought of as the basis for whatever gifts you have. If you were a spiritual person or some type of magician in a previous life, this is likely to manifest itself in this life as well. If you are able to control your mind through meditation and navigate the tricky waters of the bardo, the state between death and rebirth, you can have a great deal of control over your next incarnation. Important Tibetan lamas typically leave prophecies detailing where their next incarnation can be found. How and where these lamas incarnate is very important to their culture and politics. It was only a few years ago that the Kagyu sect of Tibetan Buddhism was troubled by two competing incarnations of the Karmapa, the head of one of the four major schools of Tibetan Buddhism. Lots of arguments and even alleged assassination attempts were involved in sorting it out.

Unless you spend a great deal of time in retreat mastering higher meditation practices such as the Six Yogas of Naropa, forget about having that kind of control over your rebirth. You can, however, use the various methods of past-life regression to investigate former lives that have impacted your current incarnation.

Of course, the ultimate test to find if you are gifted in magick and what those gifts are is simply to try it out and see how successful you are. This book gives you a set of tools with which to train yourself, but there are other programs and paths. The key is finding the right one. Whatever you do, it is vital that your training not run counter to your gifts. As an example, I once met a man who had an amazing gift for healing by touch that manifested naturally. His patients reported not only wonderful success in almost everything he tried to heal, but strange visions of swirling colors as he did it. Looking to develop his gift, he sought out Reiki attunements and training. Everything he was taught in Reiki seemed to run counter to the way he did things naturally, but he had faith in the system and stuck with it until he retrained himself to heal the Reiki way. Unfortunately, this turned him from an amazing natural healer into a just mediocre Reiki practitioner. He could hang a sign out and claim to be fully trained, but his natural gift was lost, and his success rate dropped dramatically until eventually he gave it all up. If he had found a different system of training, or relied upon his own intuition or guides, he might still be healing people today.

The previous cautionary tale is not meant to scare you away from difficult work. Real training will be tough and will at times challenge your talents and preconceived ideas. Too many people these days look for a system that reflects their current habits and proclivities rather than a system that presents difficult challenges to grow by. If, however, your training seems to be completely counterintuitive, then you should look for something else. There are many different ways of doing just about anything. A good friend of mine, who is a natural Witch, recently almost threw in the towel because the ceremonial magick that she was training in seemed to dampen, rather than enhance, her gifts. She also didn't feel any kinship with the Pagan paths of Wicca that she had encountered. Once she switched to a more open type of training, such as what I present here in this book, she seemed to thrive.

Despite the manner of your approach you may find that there are certain tasks of magick that you find extremely easy, some you will have to train hard at to develop reasonable talents, and others you may find elude you completely. I am a bit of a wiz with protective and combative Sorcery, but can't work gambling magick to save my life. Even work done by other people on my behalf seems to fizzle when it comes to gambling. A friend in New Orleans made me a gambling gris-gris bag to take to the casino and it was a complete dud until I finally handed it over to my wife. The moment it hit her hands, she pulled down a couple hundred dollars on a slot machine and kept winning all night. That's just the way it is with some things. I could perhaps spend a lot of time and energy overcoming the problem and maybe gain some success, but sometimes it's better to just go with the flow.

As you progress through the work in this book, you should take some time to investigate your gifts. Talk to relatives and find out if there are any psychics or Sorcerers in your family tree. Light a candle to the ancestors and ask them to help you awaken. Do some past life sessions with a hypnotist or just meditate on it and see if you gain any insight into yourself that way.

Most importantly, do not be ruled by what you find! This is your current life, not your great-great-grandmother's, and not whoever you used to be in 1682. They are just influences on the present. It's much more important to experiment and test what you learn. See what you are good at, what you need to work at, and where your real stumbling blocks are. Your gifts are the base of the path, but should not be allowed to define the whole experience.

NEW EDITION COMMENTARY

Nothing in this world can take the place of persistence.
Talent will not; nothing is more common than unsuccessful men with talent.
Genius will not; unrewarded genius is almost a proverb.
Education will not; the world is full of educated derelicts.
Persistence and determination alone are omnipotent.
The slogan "Press On!" has solved and always will solve the problems of the human race.

—*Calvin Coolidge*

In this chapter, I talk about gifts and how our natural gifts affect our magick. All of it is true, we all are gifted slightly differently, but I feel like I need to add that whatever your natural gifts and talents are is way less important than what you do with them. If I have to pick between someone with massive amounts of natural talent that doesn't do much practice, or someone who seems completely average at the start but is diligent and disciplined about their work—I will take the second person every time.

What this means for you is that you shouldn't focus too much on having or not having gifts. Let persistent work and practice reveal the gifts you have.

You may find that you are stronger in some areas than others. Some people don't see or hear spirits even after months of work, but every spell they cast gets the results they ask for. Others receive psychic impressions with ease, but have trouble translating magick into practical results.

Every strength or weakness presents a choice: work on it or leave it alone. It is tempting to throw our efforts into "fixing" our weak spots, but greatness often comes from accepting our weaknesses and focusing on our strengths. That said, there are some areas that you may decide you cannot ignore. I am not naturally talented at financial Sorcery. I had to work hard to gain competency and eventually mastery in that field of work. Gambling, however, is a weak area that I am happy to let stay weak.

CHAPTER 2

The Three Levels

Most ancient systems presented a view of reality consisting of various layers emanating from the highest and most subtle divine realms to the most dense and material world that we experience every day. Because the movement from the subtle to the material is not really a system of different and distinct layers but rather a seamless spectrum, you can find many ways of dividing it up. The more attention to detail you look for, the more layers you will see. Some of these systems entail dozens of layers and sub-layers, giving quite detailed descriptions of the role and potential of each. For our purposes we can rely upon a simple three-level system, such as the one presented in the Chaldean Oracles.

The Oracles are a set of 2nd-century Pagan Gnostic texts that have been an inspiration to magicians and mystics for centuries. They speak of the universe as consisting of Empyrian, Aetherial, and Material worlds. This simple system is loosely mirrored in the Celestial, Moral, and Mundane triads of the tree of life and the Dharmakaya, Sambhogakaya, and Nirmanakaya of Tibetan Buddhism.

The famous Czech magus Franz Bardon posited a similar three-world system of the Akashic, Astral, and Physical planes. Henry Cornelius Agrippa divided it up into Intellectual, Celestial, and Elementary worlds. It is important to realize that these levels exist not only as different layers of the external world, but as sheaths of our own being, each more subtle than the last. We can forsake arcane terms such as Akashic, Empyrian, and Aetheric and just call them Level One, Two, and Three.

Level One is the Empyrian, Divine, or Akashic Realm. The gods here exist in their highest and most cosmic transcendent nature. There is no hint at this level of the classic mythology that tells of fights and affairs between the gods and which sometimes make the pantheons sound like dysfunctional families. No, here we are beyond all that and dealing instead with cosmic and causal forces. Within the mind this manifests as the gnosis of non-duality and the radiance of primordial unencumbered awareness: the perfection of perfection. Level One is both the highest rung on the ladder and the material from which the ladder itself is made.

Level Two is the Aetherial Realm. It is the world of the subtle elements of pure fire, water, air, and earth. At the lower end of this level is the home of the astral body and an innumerable population of spirits. Here too is the origin of the subtle energy that has many names: prana, chi, lung, odic force, Witch-power, and so on. At the higher end of Level Two are archetypes, planetary intelligences and angels, as well as the lower mythic aspects of various gods, goddesses, and other subtle beings that despite their spiritual nature display ego clinging. Within the mind, Level Two is the realm of thought, ego, and logic. At the higher end of the spectrum are intuition, clairvoyance, and the beginnings of transcendence and transpersonal characteristics.

Level Three is the material world within which we exist. It contains within it three levels of its own: nonliving, living, and etheric substance. Nonliving substance is not only matter that we see

Real Sorcery

around us such as concrete and such, but also electricity and magnetism and other energies that can be measured with scientific instruments. Living substances include not only flesh and bone, but also bioenergy. Etheric substance acts as a bridge between Level Three and Level Two. Within the mind, this is the home of emotions and lower mechanistic thoughts and responses.

Many mystical traditions tend to ascribe a value upon the various levels, saying the material world is bad, and the subtle good. When you attain knowledge of the subtle realms this is an easy trap to fall into because it is so different from what you are used to perceiving and can seem unspeakably beautiful. This, however, is a bit of a trap. Never forget that while matter longs for the embrace of spirit, spirit strives to manifest in matter. It is okay for a mystic to shed the material for the subtle, but the Sorcerer must strive to travel freely upward and downward through the realms. A Sorcerer is concerned with not only gaining gnosis and enlightenment, but also reflecting that gnosis out into the world through magick.

As the *Emerald Tablet* states:

It ascends by means of earth into heaven and again it descends into the earth, and retakes the power of the superiors and of the inferiors.

Thus, you have the glory of the whole world.

Aleister Crowley in *Liber Tzaddi* similarly wrote:

Many have arisen, being wise. They have said, "Seek out the glittering Image in the place ever golden, and unite yourselves with It."

Many have arisen, being foolish. They have said, "Stoop down unto the darkly splendid world, and be wedded to that Blind Creature of the Slime."

I who am beyond Wisdom and Folly, arise and say unto you: achieve both weddings! Unite yourselves with both!

Beware, beware, I say, lest ye seek after the one and lose the other!

My adepts stand upright; their head above the heavens, their feet below the hells.

But since one is naturally attracted to the Angel, another to the Demon, let the first strengthen the lower link, the last attach more firmly to the higher.

THE USE OF THE LEVELS
IN MAGICK

Anyone that has taken the time to study different methods of magick that have arisen in different cultures knows that there are drastic differences in their modes of operation and different points that are stressed. Looking at these in the context of the three levels mentioned on page 12 can be very helpful in determining how a given ritual or spell works, and how it can work better.

In Hoodoo, for instance, most spells are operated by appealing directly to Level One through prayer and invocation, then channeling that directly into the Material world of Level Three in the form of oils, powders, candles, and so on. Although they do sometimes work with spirits, there is very little in Hoodoo about working with energies of the body or astral forms, so we can say that Level Two is of less concern. In Golden Dawn–style ceremonial magick, there is also an emphasis on the Empyrian Realm of Level One through prayer and invocation, but the Aetherial realms of Level Two are also very prominent in the taking of astral forms and channeling of energy through visualizations of pentagrams and such. The material component of Level Three is present in the use of specialized tools, but overall it is not as stressed as it is in Hoodoo and other types of folk magick. Certain Taoist types of magick seem to skip Level One altogether and focus on the Aetherial channeling of *qi* (energy) into material bases like talismans and such.

Some types of magick focus on one realm almost exclusively. Prayer, for instance, appeals purely to Level One, but can be amazingly powerful when done by either a gifted priest or a large group. The emerging discipline of psionics focuses almost entirely on Level Two and the manipulation of psi energy. Other disciplines like Raja yoga feature a balance of all three levels, but are focused only on individual enlightenment and have no emphasis on Sorcery.

I had never encountered a really balanced system of Sorcery until I started studying Tibetan magick. Tibet has spent as much energy throughout the last 1,200 years on magick and meditation as the rest of the world has on science and business, so it's no surprise that they have developed a system that incorporates high ceremonial techniques, intense yogic methods of channeling energy, and advanced folk magick using herbs, dolls, talismans, and the like. I am not, however, suggesting that my readers take up Tibetan magick. It is bound to a specific culture and religion so different from the Western mindset that even the Dalai Lama acknowledges that conversion can cause more problems than benefits for some Westerners. I am suggesting however that, in our Sorcery, we strive to achieve a balance of the three realms in our work.

I have from time to time been able to advise people on spells that have failed, or to witness ritual work that doesn't manifest successfully. This is almost always due to a failure of understanding the role of one of these three layers. For instance, I have seen several Pagan and ceremonial rituals raise quite a lot of Level Two energy aimed for a specific purpose, which is just sort of released at the end of the rite hoping it will hit its target. If these folks instead channeled it into a material object such as a talisman or powder that could be given to or planted near the target, it would give the energy a path to run along. Similarly, I have seen people take meticulous care with the mixing of a proper oil or mojo bag, but not make any real effort to pray fervently or channel any energy into it, and so end up with spiritually "dead" materials.

When planning a working, Levels One, Two, and Three should all be present to some degree. Level One provides wisdom and access to the non-dualistic powers that are at the very basis of reality itself. By meditation, trance, and devotional prayers, you will grow to understand the fabric of reality and thus how to bend its normal rules.

Level Two provides energies that will power your Sorcery like a battery. You can use either your own energy or the energy of anything around you, from the path of the sun, to the magnetic poles, to the stars, to the elements themselves. These can be channeled through your body like a yogi or martial artist would do, or they can be linked directly to something else and released on their own. This is also the level that is worked with to facilitate contact with spirits through evocation and offering.

Level Three will ground your magick and help it manifest physically. Even if it is only a candle or a stick of incense, adding some material component to any ritual will help it gain a foothold onto this reality. Contrary to what people in the "it's all in the mind" school of magick think, purely mental magick tends to generate purely mental results. This school of thought tends to treat any ritual components as dispensable props with no inherent value in and of themselves because magick is "all in the mind." Don't buy into it. The mind is important, but magicians, Witches, and Sorcerers meticulously recorded their formulas through the centuries for a reason. To disregard them out of hand in favor of a modern fad is just a bit disrespectful.

That's not to say that magick is not "material tolerant"; any advanced practitioner knows how to make replacements and substitutions for everything from hard-to-get herbs to golden goetic seals. However, if you do the best you can with your materials it will show in your results.

It is also important to know how the three levels play out in our own persona. As I said previously, the material level is your physical body and also the base, chemical-driven passions, which should be kept in decent shape if the more subtle energies of Level Two are to be drawn through it. Level Two is the astral body with channels, subtle winds, and seeds, as well as the higher psyche that rides upon these energies. Level One is your higher self, divine nature, and primordial awareness, the very base of your being. All three need to function in union if you are to be a successful Sorcerer. People who focus exclusively on Level Three become slaves to the base passions and physical needs. People who work only on developing the energies of Level Two or without the ennobling influences of Level One often develop various emotional problems and in rare cases physical ailments from energetic imbalances. People that work only on Level One tend to lose focus of the material world and get "lost in the clouds," so to speak.

I will close this chapter by reminding you that there are no firm barriers between the three levels; each one flows into the other. No psychic or magickal model is ever perfect. They all try to explain very profound and ineffable truths in woefully inadequate terms; the three-level model is no different. It is there to help wrap the mind around certain concepts, but the danger in every model is that it can set limits where there ought to be none. Remember the following axiom: *the menu is not the meal, the map is not the terrain.* Never confuse the description of a thing with the thing itself. This is true for all things in life, and doubly so for magick and spirituality.

NEW EDITION COMMENTARY— SEVEN LEVELS

The concept of there being different levels that magick operates on is one that I find consistently useful. Of course in reality there are no clearly defined levels. It's a spectrum that can be divided in a number of ways. The threefold division here closely mirrors what you will find in Agrippa's *Occult Philosophy*, Buddhist Vajrayana, and the Chaldean Oracles. Once you grasp this, you can start to look at more complex divisions.

The one that I find most consistently illuminating is a seven-fold division.

1. Physical: This is the hard-edged world we all know. Three dimensions of space. We experience time moving forward. Movement requires physical exertion of some kind.

2. Etheric: A layer between the physical and astral. It can't be detected by physical implements but is not entirely separate either. If you think of winds and channels in yoga or meridians in acupuncture, these are nonphysical structures that require physical exertion to affect. Breath and muscle are used in things like yoga and qigong. Needles or pressure are used in acupuncture and moxibustion.

3. Astral: Still experiencing three dimensions of space, but things are a lot more malleable. You can affect the astral through application of the will and imagination. This is why those who warn of the dangers of the astral consider it like a maze of mirrors; it can easily reflect our hopes and fears. There are multiple levels covered here, ranging from a layer that closely mirrors the physical, to lands so alien that they have almost no relation to our world. It is my belief that many different etheric and physical universes connect at this level. This is, for lack of a better term, "the other side."

4. Psycho-Noetic or Symbol Space: Just as the etheric level bridges the physical and the astral, this level bridges the astral and mental levels. It is at this level that pure information manifests into space and the higher subtler levels of astral space collapse into pure information. It is from this level that the more

effective seals, sigils, mandalas, and magickal circles come. Pure information expressed symbolically and spatially.

5. Mental: It is here that we should stop using the term "space" because there really is no spatial distance. Things simply are. In the 1800s, theosophists described this level as "the Akashic records" and conceptualized it as a library. I think a better analogy is available now: programming code. Symbol space and the astral can be thought of as websites with a graphical user interface, but underneath that is just lines of code. It's a rough analogy, but useful. In the end you need to experience this yourself.

6. Causal: At this state even the concept of subject-object starts to break down. It is a bridge between the mental level and what lies underneath everything. It is here that existence as we know it starts to, well, exist.

7. Perfection: I don't want to say much about this. Is it God? Is it Void? Is it Emptiness? Is it Fullness? By definition, it is beyond our current understanding. This is what one medieval mystic called "The Cloud of Unknowing" because it is beyond our ability to grasp.

Framing your practice in these seven layers and understanding how your magick works through this lens will make you a better Sorcerer. You will see not only how different types of spirits are oriented to different levels, but also how to bolster parts of a working so that it covers that layer more completely.

CHAPTER 3

Subtle Keys

Every ritual ever written is really a collection of words, gestures, breaths, gazes, and mental exercises that are strung together to form a whole. Similar to katas or forms taught to martial artists, these rituals serve a purpose in and of themselves, but the advanced practitioner must learn how to break them down into their component parts and use each individually. Not all Sorcery happens in the temple; a lot of magick can be done in the field, right in your home, place of business, or out in the street. Field magick doesn't always require rituals or even words. Some Sorcery can be launched while having a conversation or simply looking at someone. To be able to do this effectively, the Sorcerer or Sorceress must train to be able to cast spells with a simple gesture, a gaze, a series of breaths, or a few words spoken in a special way.

These seemingly small tricks of gaze, voice, and mind are closely guarded secrets in some occult circles. There are many rites whose words and stage directions are published openly and have secret aspects to them that are unlocked by initiates who have been passed certain keys to the performance. This chapter contains a series of subtle keys that can either be incorporated into larger rituals or used alone. Some are aimed at delivering magickal intent, some at perceiving other planes, and some are simply designed to break down your normal perception of reality and put you in a *sorcerous* state of mind.

THE BREATH

It is my opinion that a Sorcerer who cannot control his breath is no Sorcerer at all. There is a reason that in many cultures the word for spirit or energy is also the word for breath. In Hebrew the word is *ruach*, in Tibetan it's *lung*, in Sanskrit it's *prana*, in Greek it is *pneuma*, in Arabic it is *ruh*. Even the word spirit or spiritus means breath in Latin. The breath is life and is so important that it is treated in some Eastern traditions as a mantra in and of itself. Yet, we pay surprisingly little attention to it.

From the beginning, breath is neglected. Right at the moment of birth the doctor usually cuts the umbilical cord before the lungs have had a chance to clear the fluid that has built up in utero. Our first breaths in this life are breaths of panic and fear, a trauma that some say we never quite recover from, and as such we remain afraid of taking a full and complete breath out of fear.

Under normal circumstances people use only about one-seventh of their lung capacity, taking in only one pint of air, approximately fifteen times per minute. When we are excited or frightened we breathe even faster and shorter, which only heightens our state of fear. This response does, of course, have an evolutionary role in keeping us safe from danger, but in our modern world this reflex kicks in under all kinds of stress that does not involve actual danger, and in which a cooler head would be of more benefit.

The breath is an autonomic function: it happens automatically like your heartbeat and digestive function. Of all the autonomic systems, the breath is the easiest to take voluntary control of and is thus an excellent way to bridge the gap between the conscious and subconscious mind. The breath usually follows whatever state your mind happens to be in, but it's easy to reverse the process and make the mind follow the breath instead—just breathe deeply.

The Vase Breath

The first breath that we need to cover is called the vase breath because you are filling the lungs like you would fill a vase with water: from the bottom up. As I mentioned previously, the lungs will hold about seven pints of air, yet we generally draw in only one pint at a time. We also tend to favor the upper chambers of the lungs, puffing out our chests and holding in our stomachs. Although this may be a more physically attractive way of breathing, it's not very efficient. To perform the vase breath, you must make sure that your back is reasonably straight and vertical. Seated or standing doesn't matter, but do not do it lying down. Simply breathe in through the nostrils, keeping the mouth closed and filling the lower chambers of the lungs first. Allow the belly to distend as you do this. Allow the upper chambers of the lungs to fill almost all the way. Without closing off your airway, hold the breath for a moment and then exhale, releasing the upper chambers of the lungs first, and then the lower. You should aim to take in about six pints of air. If you do this correctly your breath rate should slow from about fifteen times per minute to about eight times per minute.

When the vase breath is used, the blood and brain get a better flow of oxygen, which has many benefits. One of the primary benefits is that the pituitary gland begins to function optimally. This gland not only controls all the other glands in the body, but is also the physical manifestation of the third eye and the seat of mystical vision. If you are sensitive to the energies of the body then you will also note the increased flow of vital force in the body, as well as an improved ability to direct these energies using only the breath and the will.

Nine Breaths Purification

After you have managed to perform the vase breath, you should learn to cleanse the vital channels through the Nine Breaths of Purification. To do this, draw in a deep vase breath, and as you do so consider that the air coming in is pure and cleansing. As you inhale draw your right arm up at your side so that it is held straight out; this will open up the right channel that handles solar and masculine forces. With the arm still held out at the side, bend your elbow so that your hand is in front of your face, and block your right nostril with your finger. Exhale forcefully through your left nostril, visualizing all impure energies and tendencies leaving the body through the left side. Do the exact same thing again, but using the left arm and blocking the left nostril this time, exhaling through the right nostril. Repeat the process twice more for each side, making six breaths in total.

For the last three breaths simply breathe in and out through both nostrils, cleaning out the central channel. You should again visualize pure air being inhaled and impure air being exhaled. As you exhale, lean forward as far as possible to force the last bit of air out of the channel.

The Bellows Breath

The following exercise is a quick way to increase energy in just a few seconds. I can use it instead of coffee in the morning if I have to. I have used it a lot at three a.m. when writing chapters of this very book.

The technique is simple. Take a full deep inhalation, then exhale rapid, short, sharp, forced bursts. You should be able to exhale about thirty short breaths in ten seconds. After about three breaths like this, switch back to the vase breath. As you inhale, focus on drawing the breath deep down, toward the genitals. As you exhale, move your focus up the spine to the top of the head. The vital force will follow your mind. After a few vase-style breaths in this manner, you can go back to the short, sharp, rapid exhales.

The rush that this breath technique provides is very tangible and acts as a sort of reboot for the brain. Some people have even used it to fend off cravings for cigarettes and coffee.

The Breath of Fire

This breath should be attempted only by people who have mastered all the previously mentioned breaths. It should be performed only while seated. The inhalation is performed the same way as the vase breath, but now you are going to retain the breath, condense the energy, and hold it. To do this, focus your mind on the fire seed just underneath your navel (see the Pillar and Elements practice in Chapter 4). As you inhale, the vital energy from the breath will follow the mind to the fire seed, which will grow stronger with each breath. After the inhalation, swallow a little saliva and hold your throat closed, so that you are forcing the upper winds of the body downward. Simultaneously clench your buttocks and lift upward so that the lower winds are forced upward. All this force converges on the fire center, which, in turn, fills the whole body with pure elemental fire. If you persist in the practice you will eventually feel a blissful sensation descend from the crown center, the idea being that the fire *melts* the frozen seed of wisdom.

This is actually a toned-down version of the Tibetan Tummo exercise, which has been observed to be able to raise the body temperature up to 117 degrees in laboratory conditions.[1] Without proper training and oversight, the full teaching of Tummo can be quite dangerous, but the exercise is safe for anyone who has increased their capacity through the vase breath and cleansed their channels through the purifying breath.

Pore Breathing

Pore breathing is a technique whereby you can accumulate certain energies in the body from the world around you. To perform this breath, you should imagine that your body is an empty balloon.

Perform the vase breath, but as you do, imagine that you are breathing through your skin, which is the surface of the balloon. Your whole body is a lung, inhaling and exhaling. Franz Bardon recommends scrubbing yourself in the morning with a stiff brush to open the pores. With continued practice you will actually gain the physical sensation of your skin breathing and energy passing through it; this is how you know that your visualization and physical breathing on Level One have triggered the astral response on Level Two.

If you focus your mind on particular qualities, you can draw in very specific energies such as elemental or planetary forces. The Bardonian magician Rawn Clark recommends sitting in front of a beautiful work of art and breathing in beauty itself—a wonderful practice. Throughout the book we will be requesting that you breathe in elemental, planetary, and other types of environmental energies. You can pore breathe qualities out of yourself as well. For instance, if you are feeling sluggish, you can focus on the earth element inside you and breathe it out, while breathing in the fire element. If you are feeling flighty you can exhale air and breathe in earth.

When focusing on these sources of power, I recommend focusing on the actual qualities and feel of them rather than specific symbol sets associated with various systems of correspondence. In other words, when working with the elements you would not focus on specific colors and directions, but on how these elements feel. The following table is a traditional example.

Fire	Hot	Dry	Expansive
Water	Cool	Wet	Fluid
Air	Hot	Wet	Rapid Movement
Earth	Cool	Dry	Dense and Heavy

The Loaded Breath

So far we have covered breathing mostly as it affects your own body and mind. The loaded breath takes these breath techniques into the realm of Sorcery properly, releasing the power that has been built up and targeting it at a person, object, or space. It is called the loaded breath because the breath is pregnant with whatever energy you are breathing out and patterned by your will. In the process of seducing someone, for instance, you can accumulate fire energy during the course of a conversation by gently pore breathing the fire element, patterning that energy with your desire for the target, then breathing that power directly onto the target as you talk. Just be wary of halitosis or you could counteract the whole operation!

Another example is to pore breathe the element in reverse. First accumulate it in your body and then breathe it out into a room, overloading it with that particular element. When I lived in Philadelphia, my roommate and I breathed one element into each room. By the end of the night people in the earth room were sitting like lumps on the couch watching television, people in the air room were conversing intensely about politics, people in the water room were having heart-to-hearts, and people in the fire room were making good use of the mattress. In short, they were acting out qualities related to each element.

The loaded breath is also an excellent way to bless or consecrate items as talismans for the short term. Accumulate the power that you wish to bestow and breathe it upon the item. It's a good way to cleanse an item as well. You can breathe all four elements into it, burning the impurity with fire, blowing out the fire with air, washing away the remnants with water, and finally reinfusing the item with the element earth.

You can of course use any of the above breaths in the context of larger rituals as well. For instance, you can pore breathe the proper element when doing a Golden Dawn–style pentagram ritual, or use the fire breath as a preliminary to the whole rite. Through training the energies of the body to flow with the breath you will gain better control over the powers that flow through the body and extend outward into the pentagrams.

The ways in which you can use the breath are endless. I could write an entire book on it, and perhaps one day I will, but this is enough to get you started. We must now move on from the subtle key of the breath to the magick of gazing.

GAZES

The gaze of a Sorcerer is a powerful thing. Many of the fabled magicians and Witches of old were said to be able to peer into the spirit world at a glance, or to curse someone with just their gaze alone.

The Wide Gaze

The wide gaze is a very simple technique where you simply relax your eyes and take in as much of the periphery as you can without actually changing your focus. Try for a full 180 degrees. The trick is to pay attention to everything that is happening, especially at the edges of the periphery, as it is here that you will begin to see spirits and astral forms that are out of the ordinary. You must not refocus your eyes to see what appears on the edges of vision; simply pay attention and allow the information to be processed without looking straight at it.

The Empty Gaze

The empty gaze is a slightly more radical version of the wide gaze. In the wide gaze, though you are paying attention to the full 180 degrees of vision before you, your eyes will still naturally focus on an object in front of you. The empty gaze is exactly like the 180 degree gaze, except that you will be focusing your eyes on empty space rather than letting your vision rest on a physical object.

To accomplish this, hold your finger an arm's length in front of you and focus your eyes upon it. Now withdraw your finger, but keep your eyes focused on the space where your finger was. Your eyes will want to focus on whatever objects were directly behind your finger, but you must keep your vision focused on empty space. Now, start to pay attention to the whole of your gaze as you did previously, and you will see that your perception shifts even more easily than it did before. Because your eyes are not focused on a physical object, you will find that the astral and psychic perceptions will move closer to the center of your vision and not be as difficult to perceive.

It will take a bit of work to be able to do this gaze, because the muscles in your eyes have the habit of focusing on physical objects. It may even hurt a bit, but with practice it will become second nature. In time, you will be able to shift your gaze easily whenever you want to, a useful skill when you are visiting a power spot, or for scanning someone's aura before a healing.

Dimensional Gazing

This gaze is more of a mental trick than an actual manipulation of the eyes. It is performed by taking in as much scenery in front of you as you did in the wide gaze. You don't have to worry about where your eyes are focused, just allow them to relax and take in the scene before you. Imagine that everything you are seeing in front of you is actually happening on a two-dimensional surface like a television screen. Keep gazing until you really get the sense that everything in front of you is happening on a two-dimensional surface, then reach out with your mind and contemplate what might be happening on the other side of that surface. You can even try to mentally "peel back" the two-dimensional surface, folding down a corner so that you perceive what lies beyond it.

The mind is used to perceiving space in three dimensions only. By using this gaze you are forcing the mind to perceive its usual input in only two dimensions, leaving the third dimension a vacuum to be filled by that which normally is not perceived. Practice this method often and you will find that it pays off fairly quickly in an increased perception of astral and spiritual phenomenon. If you use this gaze while looking at a scrying device like a mirror, you can consider that the mirror is a hole in the two-dimensional surface, which will allow images to surface all the more readily.

Overlooking

Just as the breath can be used to affect the mind and body of the practitioner or be projected outward to affect the world, so too can the gaze. The most famous example of this is of course the Malocchio, the Evil Eye. Belief in the Evil Eye is as widespread as it is ancient, existing in cultures all over the world and extending back all the way to ancient Sumeria. Generally speaking, the Evil Eye is given involuntarily by someone who is especially envious or furious and possesses the gift for malefica. The overwhelming spite actually overflows the channels of the subtle body and flows out through the gaze toward the target.

Of course the Evil Eye is not always given involuntarily. In England, the practice of delivering a cursed gaze was called Overlooking, Eye-biting, or Owl-blinking. The mode of delivery is essentially the same: one allows oneself to become overwhelmed with emotional force and delivers this through the gaze. The real trick to it is contained in the word "overlooking" itself. You are looking over or through the normal physical appearance of the person and into their soul, where the intent of your gaze is translated as surely as a laser reading a compact disc. It is literally a piercing gaze.

Of course the basic technique of overlooking need not be constrained to malicious intent. Love and lust can also be projected in your gaze. As long as the emotion is strong and primal, it can be projected by overlooking.

The Fascination Gaze

The fascination gaze is somewhat like overlooking except that you are not looking to pierce a person, but rather draw them into you. This is what happens when people describe being "lost" in someone's eyes. Like a fly in a spider's web they have been surrounded by the emotion of the person with whom they locked eyes.

Working with gazes is a bit hard to describe in print, but in general you want to fascinate yourself with your subject. Take in every inch and allow your mind to become obsessed with the target. You actually have to fascinate yourself in order to use this gaze. Once you are sufficiently obsessed, just mentally draw the target in with your eyes. Lock eyes for a moment and feel their gaze. Draw it in with yours. Do not think. *Feel* what you want to project. The gazes project emotion, not thought. You may be able to open someone up to telepathic suggestion using this gaze, but for the most part you want to convey emotion.

Directional Gazing

Lastly, I want to talk about directional gazing. Both occult tradition and modern psychology attribute certain qualities to looking in different directions. For instance, according to the Hevajra Tantra,[2] the gaze for overthrowing a person is to look straight at their third eye in an angry gaze, while you focus the eyes toward the left while the target or image of the target is on the left. To attract the gaze should be upward to the right with the person on the right.

Other tantric teachings say that to project wrath you should look upward with your head slightly bowed. To project calm look slightly downward. To favor analytical qualities gaze towards the left; to favor wisdom and emotion toward the right. Play with the directions of your gaze and see what qualities it evokes. There will be more about watching the gazes of others in the chapter on Influence and Persuasion.

GESTURES

The use of magickal gestures is another universal aspect of the art magickal. Be it one of the many mudras of Buddhist and Hindu magick, the Corrguineacht[3] of Ireland, to the Mano Fico and Mano Cornuto of Italy, or the Golden Dawn's "Sign of the Enterer," the coordination of the body with the movement of energy and will is a universal way of making magick. However, even while the physical gesture is well known, there are subtle mental keys and processes that do not get passed down. The following are some of the gestures that I find most useful in my magick, and which will be referenced in later chapters of the book.

The Gesture of Offering

Anyone that has ever attended an offering ceremony has surely noticed that the spirits don't usually clean up after themselves. Unless they are left out for the poor or the animals, food and other sacrificial materials are still there when the spirits are finished taking their essence. Even burnt offerings leave behind the ash; therefore we can assume that it is not the Level Three physical substance that the spirits draw sustenance from, but something at the more subtle Level Two. Although I do still believe in the power and efficacy of physical substances, you can use the following gesture to make a quick offering in a pinch.

The gesture of offering is performed by rubbing the hands together to bring the vital force into the palms, then laying the palms up as if you are holding a plate of food. You can also face the palms forward if it feels appropriate. As the heat leaves the hands, visualize clouds of offering emanating from your palms. Will the force to take on the shape of whatever is most desired by the entities that you are offering to.

The Universal Center

The universal centering is as much of a meditation as it is a gesture. Its simplicity and ease of practice do not take away from its power. It is a quick and efficient method of identifying with deity and putting you into a position of spiritual power and authority. It is as powerful as any invocation at doing so.

Sit or stand with your back straight. Make a fist with your left hand and place it over your heart. Cover it with your right hand and apply about five pounds of pressure to bring the vital energies of the body into the central channel near the heart. Perform the vase breath and consider your heart to be the very center of your being. Close your eyes and consider that your heart is the very center of the universe. Do not imagine that you are somewhere else, but that you are the center around which all creation revolves.

Just as our perception that the sun revolves around the earth is destroyed by taking a larger perspective from space, consider that from the ultimate perspective the whole cosmos revolves around the seed of spirit in the heart. Do not think that you are fooling yourself in this. You are in fact revealing a spiritual, if not cosmological, truth.

With practice, you might feel the heart center vibrate with life— the physical manifestation of the awakened Logos. If you utter a divine name, such as IAO, after this gesture, you will find it possesses an added punch.

The Rending of Space

If you know about ceremonial magick you are probably already familiar with the gesture known as "Rending the Veil." The following gesture is similar, but extends into three dimensions. It was taught to me by a mystic who studied with everyone from Sufis to Yaqui Indians. I do not know where exactly she received the instruction, but it has become a staple of my practice.

Begin by performing the Universal Centering gesture as described previously. This exercise places you mentally at the center of the cosmos, where it is at its most subtle. Rub your palms together to bring the force into the hands. Place your palms together as if in a gesture of prayer and then *insert* them into the space in front of you. Don't just make a gesture; actually feel that you are penetrating normal space with your gesture. Now slowly separate the palms and part the space in front of you. You should actually feel the pressure on the back of your hands from the resistance.

Once you have parted your hands far enough apart side to side, turn one palm up and the other down. Now split space in that direction, moving one up and one down. Once your hands are far apart vertically, turn one palm to face forward and another to face behind you. Again, split space. You should end up with one palm raised upward and facing forward and another lowered facing behind you.

What you are doing here is acknowledging three dimensions of space. Once you have done this you can mentally continue to the split in all directions. This gesture is used to make the physical space around you more subtle and malleable. It is quite useful to perform before invocations or evocations, or during just about any rite where you need to send a message to the subtle realms. It has also been used as a way of distorting normal perception of oneself, so that one can project a glamour, an idealized perception that you want people to see.

Hand Gestures

The above gestures are all fairly simple physical gestures with a lot of mental and energetic processes going on behind them. Some gestures work exactly the opposite way: they are complex physically, with almost no deliberate mental and energetic work happening at the time of their implementation. Just like the lewd "flipping the bird" to a driver that cuts you off, the gesture does the work because it is an anchor to certain powers established by tradition or prior magick.

Tibetans for instance use lots of gestures to represent specific types of offerings: flowers, water, light, and so on. These aren't based on energetic patterns, but on making the hand look like the thing represented. The Mano Cornuto or "horned hand" popular with Italian Strega and heavy metal aficionados alike is done in the same vein. The hand looks like what it represents and thus invokes that power automatically by grace of tradition.

Other hand gestures do not physically represent what they attempt to project, but are themselves ways of manipulating energy by connecting channels in the fingers in specific ways. Meditators for instance very often place their hands in a Samadhi Mudra with left hand palm-up on the lap, right hand palm-up on top of that one, and the two thumbs joined tip to tip. This cultivates deep insight. The Gyan Mudra, made with the hands on or extended past the knees, the index and thumb joined tip to tip and the other three fingers extended, cultivates sharp awareness and intellectual process.

We don't have room here to make a comprehensive list of gestures, but you should study them further and experiment with using them in different rituals. You can also create gestures of your own to represent certain ideas and ritually "seal" these gestures by consecrating them as you might a talisman. They will possess both the psychological "anchor" in the mind to what they represent and the energetic key. We will talk more about gestures and anchors later in the book.

Triangle of Manifestation

One hand gesture that deserves special mention here is the "Triangle of Manifestation." This is performed by holding the hands out side by side, palms facing each other, and touching the tips of the index finger and thumb of one hand to the index finger and thumb of the other, creating a triangle of space between the two hands.

The triangle is the archetypal symbol for manifestation because it represents the union of two giving birth to another. It also represents the three dimensions of space necessary for the universe to exist. The triangle is also a symbol that can be used to trap spirits and energy. In both the Goetia and the Tantric Phurba rituals, the triangle is used as a place to hold unruly spirits so that they can be dealt with.

To use the gesture, you can capture an image in the triangle and project will and energy into the hands, releasing it into the triangle. You can mentally visualize symbols appearing in the triangle that empower any image within. Often you will feel a sudden lightness in the hands when power sent to the hands is transferred to an object within it. A very useful gesture.

NEW EDITION COMMENTARY— ACCUMULATING SUBTLE KEYS

In this chapter I focus on different beathing techniques, gestures, and gazes, but the concept of subtle keys can be taken much further than this. Any kind of short element of magick that can be done by rote in a variety of situations can become one of your subtle keys.

Words and phrases of power make excellent subtle keys. I remember once I was in the Cave of Kelpius, the first American Rosicrucian, where I felt the presence of a whole group of spirits quite strongly. I called to them in more or less plain language, praising them and asking for them to reveal themselves to me. I could feel them, but it felt like there was a divide between us, so I spoke a phrase that I have had memorized since I was a teenager:

Ati me peta babka!

This phrase is Sumerian for "Gatekeeper, open your gates to me!" I then performed the rending of space and uttered another phrase:

Peta babkama luruba anaku!

This means, "Open the Gate, that I may enter." I felt my own efforts to rend space were met by beings on the other side of that divide and I was finally able to hear a voice and make contact.

Why Sumerian? It's a sacred human language, one of the first. That's not the real importance, though, and certainly a cave just outside of Philadelphia doesn't require Sumerian words to enter. The real importance is that it marked that moment, and whatever else I did in that moment, as sacred and special. This has an effect on our own minds and energy as well as on the spirits that we are surrounded by.

There are bits of Enochian calls, fragments of Latin prayers, Sanskrit Dharinis, and more Greek phrases than I can count that have proven useful to me time and time again when either constructing larger rituals in English or working on the fly. It is not necessary to have every ritual you do committed to memory, but when the power suddenly goes out, or a mysterious wind blows the script outside the circle, you should be able to rely upon these subtle keys and your own ingenuity to handle business.

Gazes, breaths, gestures, phrases, visualizations, mental exercises, and even ritual fragments can all become subtle keys. Anything short, that you can do by rote, and that has a big impact counts as a subtle key. Over the years you will collect dozens of these and use them time and time again.

CHAPTER 4

Regular Practice

Baseball players, boxers, and gymnasts don't spend all their time competing at their sports; a large amount of time is spent working out and doing drills. Policemen, firemen, and even computer programmers have to practice what they do regularly to keep their skills sharp. Any vocation worth anything has a skill set that must be learned, developed, and maintained by regular exercises and practice. Sorcery is no different. In fact, because magick relies upon subtle senses and skills that most of humanity doesn't even acknowledge the existence of, it takes quite a lot of training, study, and practice to do it well.

In Chapter 2, we spoke about the various levels of reality and how they come together to make magick. In this chapter, I present some exercises that you should incorporate into regular practice to strengthen your body, your mind (as it can exist in the three levels), and to increase your ability to channel the powers that you will handle in your work as a Sorcerer.

MEDITATION

If I had to give up all magickal and spiritual disciplines except one, I would happily ditch every invocation, spell, and exercise that I know in favor of simple meditation. Meditation is the key to the system of magick in this book and will assist you in any other systems of magick or spirituality that you will ever engage in. Indeed, it will assist and enhance just about any human endeavor whatsoever. I cannot stress its importance enough.

Why is meditation so important? Because, whether you realize it or not, ninety-nine percent of everything that you think and everything you do is not a result of your own conscious choice, but a mechanistic and programmed response. We like to believe that everything we think and do emanates from our own conscious will, but it is not true. Almost all thought and action are really just a reaction triggered by innumerable changing factors. Even most of what we consider the "self" is just layers upon layers of programming and habit.

Consider for a moment how different your thoughts and actions and, indeed, your *self* would be if you were given a frontal lobotomy. Pretty huge change, right? Obviously that is very drastic, but how about if I fed you LSD? How much of what you would think and do is affected by that? How about a few martinis? How about a Red Bull? I drank a triple espresso about an hour before I wrote this sentence. Had I had a chamomile tea instead there is a very good chance that this paragraph would have come out differently.

What you had for breakfast, the quality of the air, your drive to work, how you are dressed, how you were raised, how many siblings you have, how popular you were in high school, the genetics you inherited from your parents, the random firing of synapses in the brain—these are just a few of the millions of factors that impact every moment of every day, and we all spend most of our time being pushed and pulled by them. Causes and conditions have, from the moment we were born, programmed us to be certain ways, and most of the time we follow that programming as surely as a machine does. Thus the term "mechanistic mind."

When someone yells at us, for instance, all that is physically happening is that someone is making vibrations in the air that we interpret as sound. How we react to that sound should be our conscious choice, but if we are honest we will have to admit that it's usually not. It's like someone shooting an arrow at your heart, but which falls short at your feet. Rather than leaving it there and walking away, you pick it up and plant it in your own chest. Imagine if you could simply leave it there and choose your next action consciously without being a slave to the push and pull of the mechanistic mind.

Another example is to pretend that you come home to find a window in your house has been broken with a rock. You would probably be furious, and understandably so. It might even ruin your whole day. Now imagine that you had won several million dollars before arriving home to find the broken window. It's probably not going ruin your day, right? But why? The two are really unconnected and shouldn't have anything to do with each other, but because we act primarily from mechanistic reaction rather than conscious action our response is locked in by prior causes and conditions.

The Russian mystic G. I. Gurdjieff used to call this the prison. If you are in prison, your first duty should be to escape. But how? It helps to have others who also are working to escape, thus the need for spiritual communities, magickal orders, and the like. Even more important is outside help, especially if it's from people who have themselves escaped the prison and can guide you out. This is where teachers and instruction come into it, especially with regard to meditation.

Now let me clarify for a moment what I mean by meditation, because meditation can mean plenty of things. The word itself is defined only as "to engage in mental exercise for spiritual purposes," which covers a lot of ground. So while technically kneeling in prayer, doing tai chi, or lying on the bed and listening to Enya could be considered meditation, they are not what I mean by meditation.

What I mean by meditation is a process for alleviating the grasping at thoughts and cutting through mental distractions through single-pointed focus. There are many methods for this. The one I teach below is called the Gate of Heka.

THE GATE OF HEKA MEDITATION

Sit in a chair or on a cushion in your favorite asana[1] with your back straight. Begin your session with the nine purification breaths, releasing all tension and thoughts of the past, present, and future. Following that, breathe slowly and naturally and relax.

Focus your attention on the point in between your inhalation and exhalation. The breath is like a pendulum swinging back and forth. The moment that a pendulum changes direction is a magickal moment. It is not moving this way or that, nor is it at rest. It is frozen in the eternal present. Similarly when the breath is neither inhaled nor exhaled nor held is a moment outside of time called the Gate of Heka. Heka means *beyond* in Greek. In this case the moment between breaths is like a gate, through which you can pass beyond normal consciousness.

Focus your attention on this moment as you breathe. Don't stalk it like a cat stalks a mouse. Enter into it. The past is a memory. The future is a projection. The present disappears before it can be grasped. Just allow the mind to be gently aware of every moment the breath changes direction. Relax completely during the inhale and exhale. Let thoughts arise and set with no attachment.

If you are like most people you will find that distractions arise nearly instantly. Once you recognize that you have left the meditation and are distracted with a train of thought, you should simply return to the breath without chastising or criticizing yourself. In fact you should have no expectation whatsoever about how well your meditation goes. Lust of result is the biggest obstacle to meditation. Recognize that thoughts emanate from nothing and dissipate into nothing. Rest in the breath and in primordial awareness.

In all likelihood you will, at first, spend most of your meditation session doing little but being distracted, recognizing it, and returning to the breath only to be distracted again. Many of my students that find themselves in this situation claim that they can't meditate and give up. What they don't realize is that they *are* meditating. They are training their minds to recognize when it is not acting according to their will, and bringing it back from distraction.

The same meditation can be performed using just about anything as a focus. You can focus on the breath itself if that is easier than the moment between breaths. You can set up an image such as a yantra or statue to meditate upon. You can repeat a mantra and absorb your attention in that. The possibilities are endless. Pick a method that works for you and stick with it.

In the end, all methods of meditation are only ways of entering *contemplation*: the open and empty primordial state of awareness. The method gives way to awareness and can be dropped in favor of luminous clarity. Like a lake whose waters have been still, all the clouds of dirt will settle and reveal the mind's natural clarity. Thoughts may arise within the field of awareness, but you will not feel overly attached or averse to any of them. Just as a mirror can reflect flowers or dog shit without attachment or aversion, your mind will be able to operate in the same way toward its contents.

Do not shoot for long sessions right away. Start with just twenty minutes in the morning right after you get up, and twenty minutes right before bed. These two twenty-minute sessions should be tied together by lots of "meditative moments" throughout the day: a minute or so of focusing on the breath and cutting through distraction. This can be done anywhere at any time. At your desk, in a restaurant, or on the toilet are all acceptable places. If you practice in this way, you will definitely see a difference in your life in a relatively short period of time.

So why is this so important in Sorcery? Simple: being an effective Sorcerer is all about attaining your will. First you have to know what your will is. If you are forever chasing after whims that are generated by advertisements, or continuing counterproductive patterns of behavior, then you will never know your will, and thus never be a successful Sorcerer. You can do all the magick in the world to attract money or love, but unless you are able to override some of the programming that has limited your success thus far, your magick won't help very much. Furthermore, if you are going to speak with the spirits you will need to be able to cleanse your mind, just to give them room to speak. Then you need to be able to recognize thoughts that stem from your own mind and those that are real communications. This is the kind of result that can be attained only by hard work and regular practice.

OFFERINGS

The practice of making offerings comes in as a close second to meditation as far as practices that I place importance upon. Some of the oldest and most powerful systems of magick and religion are literally built around nothing but the practice of making the right offerings to the right powers. If you get into the habit of making offerings regularly to the spirits and powers that be, not only will your Sorcery be more effective, but many other endeavors will receive an added boost, or seem aided by a helpful unseen hand.

The benefit of offerings is best explained in real-world terms. If you and I just met, and I suddenly asked you to lend me $100, you would probably not loan it to me because you don't know me. If I asked my coworker for the same loan, he would be a bit more likely to loan me the money because he knows me better and has an easy way to find me. He would, however, want to know a firm date to expect his repayment. My best friend, by comparison, would loan me the money no questions asked. In fact, he would probably offer more money just to make sure I was covered. He wouldn't worry much about the date of repayment because we have decades of history together and this would be just another example of the give and take between close friends.

By making offerings to the ruling powers, local spirits, and even to the land and sky, you are building a relationship, just like a relationship between two people. The older and more firm your relationship with the universe, the more apt it is to help you out when you need it. By serving the local spirits of your area, you will gain allies that will not only respond when summoned but also act on your behalf of their own accord. When you start doing a spell, the powers that be will be ready to respond with boons that can at times exceed expectations. Indeed there have been times when spirit familiars of mine have seemed to respond even to casual statements made in jest to friends of mine. That's how I learned how important it is that when you do get that friendly with spirit beings, you set up clear rules for your interaction.

On the other side of the coin, not all spirits are friendly. Some are naturally wrathful. Others act in retribution for actions that we take that have consequences in spiritual dimensions, such as polluting, building in power places, or even doing magick that is counter to the nature of the place where we do it. Offerings are a pacifying practice that protects by offering an olive branch to hostile spirits and elemental forces. A large part of the Shaman's role in traditional cultures deals with mending these harmful breaches and smoothing out the relationship between this world and the next. By making offerings, we are sending a signal to those forces that any breaches were accidental and that we are attempting to make reparations.

As to what is offered, there are many types of offerings that can be made, both physical and emanated from the Sorcerer in the astral.

Though some rare and potent spirits will be able to devour the physical offerings, most beings feed upon the subtle essence of the physical offerings rather than the substance itself. The exception to this are burnt substances of fumigation. There are many spirits who can take nourishment directly from the smoke produced by burnt herbs, plants, and woods. Even if one uses physical offerings, such as cakes and alcohol, one should multiply these offerings through force of will and see them filling infinite space and taking the shape of whatever is desired.

Offerings need not be done ceremoniously or formally. You can leave a dime or some whiskey on a grave, lay some flowers or pour some water near a tree or plant, or burn some incense in the backyard, mentally offering it to the ten directions. You can also use the Gesture of Offering from the last chapter to emanate an offering of your own energy directly. Acts of generosity like this, no matter how small, serve to build up a good relationship with the spiritual forces around your home and wherever you travel.

If you do want to make a formal ritual offering, below is a ritual that is short enough to be done regularly. The physical support for the offerings will be some incense or a burnt wood such as juniper or sandalwood. If you are doing the rite outside, you can add to this some water, tea, or whiskey to spill on the ground as a libation. Because you are making offerings to spirits that may initially be hostile to you, I recommend staying away from herbs that aid in the manifestation of spirits such as Dittany of Crete or mullein. I call the incense a "physical support," because you will be feeding that incense with energy directly, visualizing it filling all space, and willing it to take on whatever shape is most pleasing to the recipient.

If you want to make more elaborate physical offerings, especially ones directed at specific classes of spirits, be very careful in what you offer. Research the traditions carefully and then use that knowledge to make an appropriate offering. Then listen to the spirits and see if they ask for something specific. Some offerings, like meat or musk to

Nagas and salt to spirits of the dead, can actually offend a guest and make the ritual counterproductive. If you aren't sure of what you are doing, stick to the gesture of offering and simple substances such as incense and liquor.

Rite of General Offering

Take your incense and your libation if you have one, and arrange them on an altar or table. Don't light the incense yet. Hold your hands over the offerings, forming the triangle of manifestation between your hands. Say the following:

> By Earth, the Body of the Gods
> By Water, their flowing blood
> By Air, the breath of the Gods
> By Fire, their burning soul
> May these offerings be made blessed and made pure.

As you say this, consider that any impurities in the offerings are washed, blown, and burned away. Say the following:

> Spirits of the firmament of earth and of ether
> Spirits of the dry land and of the flowing water
> Spirits of the whirling air and of the rushing fire
> Come! Come!

Phantoms of the dead, the quick, and in-between
To those whom I owe debt and who owe debt unto me
Famulus and guardians who are bound unto me!
Come! Come!
Every dryad, sylph, and satyr who dwells within this place
Every undine and salamander, every fey and gnomish spirit!
Every succubi and incubi, every spectre of ill will
Come! Come!
All spirits who cause help or harm in response to human
    action!
Come here according to your desires, be seated on the
    thrones
Io evohe! Come! Come!

Light the incense. Give the gesture of offering. Say the following:

Clouds of offerings, I give to you
Food and drink and fumigation
Enjoy! Enjoy!
Let the offerings arise and pervade all space
Let it take the form that is most desired
Enjoy! Enjoy!
Friends and family from former lives
I am grateful for your past kindness
Enjoy! Enjoy!
You who form obstacles as retribution
Forgive offences made by mistake or delusion
Enjoy! Enjoy!
Spirits of the dead and trapped in between spaces
Wardens of this ground and keepers of the winds
Enjoy! Enjoy!
Guardians and familiars, be fulfilled
Quickly realize my hopes and desires
Enjoy! Enjoy!

To each of you I offer inexhaustible treasures
Delightful substance, and enjoyments.
You who would harm me
Partake of this feast and be at peace
You who would help me
Be fulfilled and accomplish that with which you are
    charged

After making this charge, you can either go directly on to the closing, or sit and try to commune with the forces invoked. Use some of the gazes to scan your surroundings. Say the following:

Honored guests of this temple, the window of our commu-
    nion is closing
Take your last taste of these enjoyments and go in peace.
Vacate the thrones of the feast and go forth unto your
    abodes and habitations as you desire
Forever act as friends and helpers
As you came in power, go in peace
Ite Missa Est

INVOCATION

Invocation is a specific type of prayer. Rather than praying for blessings, however, an invocation is focused on uniting your mind with the mind of a deity or power. Later in the book I will give plenty of invocations that focus on channeling specialized power such as Jupiterian power for business and Venusian power for love, but there is something more important that I need to give first: the invocation of the Divine itself (which is both the Logos within you and the Pleroma without). At the ultimate level, there is no difference between the two.

The following is a slightly altered invocation from the Stele of Jeu in the Greek Magickal Papyri (PGM). The invocation was originally used as an exorcism and invoked the "Headless One." The Golden Dawn and Aleister Crowley versions changed this to the "Bornless One," which, while not an accurate translation, I think strikes closer to the original meaning as the invocation calls upon the most ultimate and infinite divinity beyond all conception of space and time. The individual is then identified as inseparable from that divinity, awakening the Logos or divine spark within. The original can be found in PGM V 96-172. The Crowley version can be found in his *Liber Samekh.*

Apart from awakening the Divine within, it can also be used to attain what is known as the knowledge and conversation of your Holy Guardian Angel. This angel is a very special being about which there is much controversy. The term originates from the grimoire *The Sacred Magick of Abramelin,* which details an eighteen-month operation to make contact with an angel that is specifically bound to you. The nature of this angel is a hotly debated topic amongst occultists. Some see it as a sort of higher self. Others see it as a totally separate being. My own experience is that it is a bit of both.

Once you attain the knowledge and conversation of the Holy Guardian Angel, or as I like to call it, the Agathodaimon (good spirit), you can decide for yourself. The angel will act not only as a guide for you on the path, but also as a type of fetch that assists in summoning and controlling various spirits and powers to you. As to how long it takes to make contact, I personally don't think you can time it. The original German versions of Abramelin prescribe eighteen months.[2] Samuel Liddell MacGregor Mathers mistranslated it as six months, yet people have gotten success with this mistranslation. It took me a bit longer than that, it takes others far less. It really depends upon your own capacity and the spiritual work you have done up until that point in both your present incarnation as well as former lives.

The version of this invocation given in *Liber Samekh* is one that Crowley used to attain Knowledge and Conversation. The version that I give here is the version that I used to attain mine.

Real Sorcery

Invocation of the Bornless One

AOTH ABRAOTH BASYM ISAK SABAOTH IAO

I summon thee the Bornless One

Thee that didst create the earth and the heavens

Thee that didst create the night and the day

Thee that didst create the darkness and the light

Thou art OSORONNOPHRIS whom no man hath seen at any time.

Thou art IABAS

Thou art IAPOS

Thou hast distinguished between the just and the unjust

Thou hast made the female and the male

Thou hast revealed the seed and the fruit

Thou hast made men to love one another and to hate one another

I am thy prophet unto whom thou didst transmit thy arcana, the whole quintessence of Magia

Thou didst produce the moist and the dry and that which nourishes all created life.

I am the messenger of OSORONNOPHRIS!

This is thy true name handed down to the prophets.

ARBATHIAO REIBET ATHELEBERSET ARA BLATHA ALBEU EBENPHI CHI CHITASGIE IBAOTH IAO

Hear me and make all spirits subject unto me so that every spirit of the firmament and of the ether, upon the earth and under the earth, on dry land and in the water, of whirling air and rushing fire, and every spell and scourge of god may be obedient unto me.

I call upon thee with an empty spirit, oh awesome and invisible god.

AROGOGOROBRAO SOCHOU MODORIO PHAL-RCHAO OOO

Hear me and make all spirits subject unto me so that every
spirit of the firmament and of the ether, upon the earth
and under the earth, on dry land and in the water, of
whirling air and rushing fire, and every spell and scourge
of god may be obedient unto me.

Holy Bornless One hear me

ROUBRIAO MARI ODAM BAABNA BAOTH ASS
ADONAI APHNIAO ITHOLETH ABRASAX
AEOOY

Hear me and make all spirits subject unto me so that every
spirit of the firmament and of the ether, upon the earth
and under the earth, on dry land and in the water, of
whirling air and rushing fire, and every spell and scourge
of god may be obedient unto me.

MABARRAIO IOEL KOTHA ATHERE BALO
ABRAOTH

Hear me and make all spirits subject unto me so that every
spirit of the firmament and of the ether, upon the earth
and under the earth, on dry land and in the water, of
whirling air and rushing fire, and every spell and scourge
of god may be obedient unto me.

AOTH ABRAOTH BASYM ISAK SABAOTH IAO!

He is the lord of the gods!

He is the lord of the world!

He is the one whom the winds fear!

He is the one who made all things by the command of his
voice!

Lord, King, Master, Helper, empower my soul.

IEOU PYR IOU PYR IAOT IAEO IOOU ABRASAX
SABRIAM OO YY AY OO YY ADONAI

IDE EDE Good messenger of God!

ANLALA LAI GAIA DIACHARNA CHORYN

At this point perform the centering exercise. This involves placing your left fist over your heart and covering it with your right hand, applying about five pounds of pressure. Contemplate silently for a moment that your heart is at the very center of the universe. I don't mean to imagine that you have left your room, and are now somewhere out in space, but rather that the very place that you stand is the center of the entire universe. Just as from our perspective here on earth it seems that the sun revolves around us, but from a larger perspective the earth is revealed to revolve around the sun, you should consider that from an even larger perspective, you are at the very center of the universe and the whole thing revolves around you. Your heart and the universal heart are one. From this perspective, you can now utter forth the rest of the invocation.

> I am the Bornless One with sight in the feet, strong in the
>   immortal fire!
> I am the truth that hates that evil is wrought in the world!
> I am the one that makes the lightning flash and the thun-
>   der roll!
> I am the one whose sweat is heavy rain which falls upon
>   the earth, making it fertile.
> I am the one whose mouth is utterly aflame! I am the
>   destroyer and begetter!
> I am the grace of the Aeon!
> The Heart Girt with a Serpent is my name!
> Come forth and follow me so that every spirit of the fir-
>   mament and of the ether, upon the earth and under the
>   earth, on dry land and in the water, of whirling air and
>   rushing fire, and every spell and scourge of god may be
>   obedient unto me.
> IAO SABAOTH!

Despite Crowley's attempts at stabbing at the meanings of most of the words using Gematria, the majority of the words are merely divine names of power and have no firm translation. Consider them all names of the highest power. After the power is invoked in the second person, the invocation shifts to first person and you identify your own being with the divine.

The previous invocation can be a bit of a mouthful and take a bit of time to perform. If you are pressed for time, but want to perform a similar invocation, I have also used the following invocation to great success. I have found it is most potent when performed in Greek, so I include it here in its original language.[3]

Invocation of the Agathodaimon

Orkizo Kretera Theou Plouton KateXonta!
(I conjure the Divine Cup [grail of God], which holds all
   things!)
Orkizo Theon Aionion Aiona te Panton!
(I conjure the god of Aeons, Aeon of all!)
Orkizo Physin Autophye, Kratison Adonaion!
(I conjure self-generated nature, mighty Adon-Aion!)
Orkizo Dynonta kai Antellonta Eloaion!
(I conjure the descending and ascending powers Elo-Aion!)
Orkizo te hagia kai Theia Onomata tauta!
(I conjure these sacred and divine names!)
Opos an pemphosi moi to Theion Pneuma!
(That you send to me the divine Spirit!)
Exe me synistamanon!
(Give me union!)
Aposteilon moi ton idion angelon te nykti
(Send to me my own angel in this night!)
Epikaloumai se hagie angele!
(I invoke you, sacred angel!)
Elthe kai parasta eis tende ten kreian kai synergeson!
(Come and give help in this operation, and synergize!
   [i.e., unite!])

THE PILLAR AND THE SPHERES

The following exercise is designed to assist you in channeling power through your body and breaking it down into different patterns, in this case the five elements. The four classical elements are of course fire, air, water, and earth. To these a fifth is often added called "spirit" or "space." Personally I find both terms to be somewhat limiting and prefer to use the old alchemical term "Azoth" for the fifth element, which should be understood to have connotation of consciousness pervading all space. Azoth can be thought of almost as clear light, which, when it hits a prism, divides up into lights of various colors. The more complex the prism, the more varied the colors. In this case, we break Azoth down into the four classical elements, but could just as easily break it down into the seven planetary energies, three gunas, and so on.

The following exercise establishes a column of energy in the body that flows between the ouranic, or heavenly, realms above, and the chthonic, or underworld, realms below. The descending energy is purifying, symbolized by the dove. The ascending energy is atavistic and vitalizing, symbolized by the serpent. After the column is established, we break the elements down into five centers or spheres in the body. The locations of the elements in the body are taken from Tibetan exercises, and while they do correspond to various chakra points, you should resist the temptation to view this exercise in the light of other chakra exercises that you may know until you have mastered this exercise in its own right.

THE PILLAR

This exercise can be done sitting or standing, and both positions should eventually be mastered. In either case, the back should be held as straight as possible and you should again center yourself with vase breaths and perform the Universal Centering exercise from the last chapter.

Take a deep inhalation and imagine that above you, emanating from the highest heavens, descends a column of pure white light. This light enters the crown of your head and passes through you, down into the ground. This white light is enabling and purifying. Exhale and intone the following:

Descendat columba! (The descent of the dove!)

Take another deep inhalation and imagine that a reddish-colored light from beneath you rises through the column and passes through you upwards. Whereas the white light was purifying, this light is vivifying. As the descending light was ennobling, this energy is atavistic. Exhale and intone the following:

Ascendat serpens! (The ascent of the serpent!)

Inhale and feel the two energies entering into you from above and below. Exhale and feel the two energies flow throughout your body, impregnating every cell of your being with their power. Feel your connection between earth and sky, underworld and heavens.

THE SPHERES

Now turn your attention to the crown of your head. Imagine an empty sphere that extends above and inside your physical head. Breathe in and see a clear energy fill this sphere. It corresponds to the element AZOTH and brings increased clarity and spacious awareness. Sound the name IAO (EE AH OH). Move the mind downward and see a sphere at the throat. Breathe in an airy, bright-yellow energy that feels warm and wet like humid air and moves about rapidly within the sphere. Sound the name IAO again to activate the sphere of air. Move the mind downward again to a sphere at the heart. Breathe in a deep-blue energy that feels cool and wet and fluid. After the sphere is filled with elemental water, sound the name again: IAO. Move the mind downward to a sphere just below and behind the navel near the base of the spine. Breathe a red, hot, dry, and expansive energy into this sphere. Sound again the name IAO. Move the mind downward again to the perineum between the legs, behind the genitals. See a dark, earth-tone energy fill this sphere that is dense, cool, and dry. When the sphere is filled, sound the name again: IAO.

Rest the mind a few minutes and contemplate the elements within the body.

The purpose of this exercise is first to energize the central and most important energy channel of the body that runs from the crown of the head to the genital area, by relating it to the universal axis of spirit descending and ascending. Then we balance the five elements along the channel, which not only mends energetic imbalances that can cause various physical and emotional ills, but also sets them up in a specific alchemical order. You could imagine the classical view of a Witch's cauldron or alchemical vial within the body. The earth is the ground that the fire is built upon. The fire boils the water in the cauldron or vial above it. The boiled water releases steam into the air. The steam ascends to the heavens and dissipates into space.

There are an array of internal energy exercises that are built upon this pattern, but for now, it is enough to master the method and be able to isolate and manipulate the different elements that you want to work with.

Once you have the exercise down, you can practice moving different energies around the body through the force of will and breath. Move them up the back and down the front, or from side to side. Focus on concentrating different elements into the hands or feet. Eventually you should practice projecting them outward into objects or even impregnating whole rooms with a specific element. Link this practice to the breathing techniques from the previous chapter and experiment. You will find endless applications.

If you practice the Pillar and Spheres daily, I can almost guarantee that you will feel a difference in a very short time. People that use this and other exercises like it begin to feel the pillar as surely as they do their own spine, even to the point that their posture changes naturally because the energies make holding the body straight more comfortable than slouching.

TIMING

Now that we have a few exercises to practice regularly, the question must be asked: how regular? Some of you are probably thinking that doing all these rituals daily would take hours and essentially be impossible to maintain with your regular schedule. I assure you it's all very doable. How often you practice it is up to you.

Not including any spells and rituals that are aimed at specific outcomes, I usually spend at least an hour a day on regular practice. On busy days, I may cut things down drastically to just twenty minutes or so. On days that I have time, I may devote two to three hours to practice. To many people, that's quite a lot of time. To others, that's not a lot of time at all. In all cases, you get out of it what you put into it. I have witnessed the notorious Ngakpa[4] Kunzang Dorje

Rinpoche do things with magick so unbelievable that I won't even print them here because you wouldn't believe it unless you saw it yourself. He could do those things because he has spent most of his life in continuous practice. Literally years at a time with very little sleep or food. You get out of it what you put into it.

I recommend first and foremost that everyone meditate, at least once, for twenty minutes, every day. Meditation is the key to magick; I cannot stress this enough.

I further recommend that you perform one of the invocations daily, even twice daily, until you attain the knowledge and conversation of the Agathodaimon, in whatever manner it reveals itself to you. The trick to this is to perform the invocation as if you are calling a spiritual lover, which indeed you are. Perform it with passion and longing for enlightenment. You will know it when you have it, but don't expect it to manifest the same way as anyone else's. After you have attained the Knowledge and Conversation, or felt that the divine spark within you has awakened, then you may feel that you need to do the formal invocation only once a week or so. Once you internalize the practice, you can incorporate it into your meditation practice.

The Pillar and the Elements should also ideally be done daily, but if you can't swing it, then do it whenever you can. If you do the spoken parts of the practice internally, or as a whisper, you may find that you can complete the practice in unexpected places. I travel for work a lot and have done it while in parking lots, on the beach, or even while walking.

Though many books recommend keeping a regular schedule for all your practices, doing them in the same place and time every day, I do not. I prefer to let my regular practice be as dynamic as my life. Sometimes I focus more on meditation, sometimes I focus more on invocation, and sometimes I focus more on the Pillar and Elements.

Offerings are the exception to this. Just like feeding pets or children, offerings should be kept to a regular schedule so that a relationship can be built between you and the spirits. If you can't do it daily, then try for once a week. If you can't swing that, then even once a month has some benefit. I myself do very truncated and silent offerings every morning and evening that take no more than a few moments. Once a week I perform the more elaborate rite given above, and several times a year I do a very elaborate ritual with many physical offerings made to please specific spirits that I work with. I also do offerings a few times a year in special places such as a graveyard that hold the bodies of some spirits that I work with, and certain power spots near where I live.

With the exception of meditation, with diligent practice, some practices can be internalized to the point where you can perform them in the span of just one breath. Recently a student who had been performing the Golden Dawns LBRP came to me for help with her practice because it had grown stale. After observing her, I noted that she had clearly internalized the ritual, and asked her to try to perform it at the speed of thought and seal it with just one word: AMEN. She was surprised by the result, which freed her up to practice some other things that she had become interested in.

In the end, you must establish your own schedule according to your own needs and situation. Some people need to do things silently and fast, so as not to alert people they share a room with. Others may have very little time because they are raising children. Others may have all the time in the world to spend in their temple as long as they wish.

RETREATS

Apart from your regular practice, I also suggest scheduling retreats for yourself. A retreat is simply a vacation from your regular life and responsibilities, where you can focus on your magick. They can last anywhere from a weekend to several years. Most people will be able to do a weekend a year, and perhaps a full week every few years.

During your retreat you can focus on mastering one practice, or simply focus on rotating between many practices. It is helpful if you can actually travel away from home. Even if you can manage to stop people from interrupting you while doing a retreat at home, there is a psychic benefit from being physically away from your normal life for a while. The distance literally makes a difference. If you can perform your retreat at a power spot or sacred site then all the better.

You can make great strides in power and realization through retreat practice. It is an especially good way to learn a new practice in a short amount of time. When you return to your regular schedule of practice that fits around your normal activities, you will notice a marked difference.

The practices given previously are really just examples. You can choose other similar practices to use instead of these. There are thousands of years of tradition throughout hundreds of cultures from which you can learn meditation, invocation, offering, and energy work. At a certain point you will feel guided to create your own rituals; this will mark your transition from novice to adept. Do not rush it, though. Many people rush to create their own rites, or experiment with as many different rituals as they can just for the sake of experimentation without ever really delving in deeply. Dilettantism is the mark of an amateur.

Be attentive to your practice, and your practice will be attentive to you.

NEW EDITION COMMENTARY— REGULAR PRACTICE

Regular practice is what distinguishes a Sorcerer from a regular person that picks up a spell book and tries a recipe or two. I think that no matter what practice you choose, you should make sure that you are covering certain areas. Meditation will make sure that you know your own mind, which is vital when we are asking it to stretch in ways it is not used to, and also when we might be hearing voices echo in our minds that are not our own. Regular offerings will keep you connected to the gods and guardians and build good rapport with the local spirits. Invocations make sure that you maintain spiritual authority and ability to speak to the universe in a way it understands. Energetic practices will ensure that your whole body is involved in your magick.

Be aware that while you may choose different rituals and exercises, they are not all the same. Even ones that look similar on the surface may prove very different in their effect. Since this book was written, numerous people have told me that they don't need to do Pillar and Spheres work because they do the Middle Pillar ritual as laid out by Israel Regardie. Both rituals involve visualizing light moving through a central pillar and activating spheres, so they must be the same, right? No. Not at all. To think so is like saying that a double cheeseburger and a tuna fish sandwich are the same thing. Both are sandwiches, but they are otherwise completely different.

The Middle Pillar ritual aligns the Sephirot of the Tree of Life onto the body to prepare you for Kabbalistic work. The Pillar and Spheres ritual in this book aligns the five elements onto the body to create an alchemical reaction. The earth at the base is consumed by the fire below the navel. The fire heats the water at the heart. The heart releases steam, which causes the air element to rise. The rising energy that contains all the elements below it melts the wisdom of space/spirit at the crown and causes it to descend. Not only does it matter that it is *elements* and not Sephirot, or planets, or chakras, but also the *order* in which the elements are stacked matters. You can stack them differently for different effects. This is the alchemy of sublimation—making your body and mind more sublime. Those interested in taking this process further can look at different styles of inner heat practice and will find themselves well-prepared energetically by this work.

Part Two
Strategic Sorcery

CHAPTER 5

Divination and Intelligence Gathering

We live in the age of information. Some of the most successful businesses on the planet are concerned with providing not material goods and services to their customers, but information. Not only is the presentation of information big business, so too are the storing, sorting, converting, protecting, processing, transmitting, and retrieving of information. The most advanced machines on the planet are dedicated to nothing more than the processing of information. Today's armies are increasingly interested in the evolving field of Information Operations, which are dedicated to the methods of disabling or corrupting their enemies' information systems. Given the overwhelming importance of information in the modern world, it only makes sense to begin our strategies with a discussion of the mantic arts: the magick of information.

Divination is the most commonly performed type of magick on the planet, and any of us who have ever read our horoscope in the newspaper, shaken a Magic 8 Ball, or predicted bad luck when a black cat crossed our path has engaged in it on one level or another. Thousands of psychics and readers are consulted every day, all over the world, by people from all walks of life, on topics ranging from lost loves to matters of state. It has been so since the beginning of human history. The Chinese have been using I Ching since 1000 BCE, making it one of the oldest types of divination on the planet. Babylonian kings, Roman generals, and even a pope have relied upon haruspices to read the livers of sacrificed animals before battle. The Bible mentions several examples of casting lots for readings that would indicate the will of God. Of course the Bible is a common tool for divination, as are the holy books of many other religions.

Ancient Greeks relied upon oracle priestesses, who would become mouthpieces for the gods. Tibetans rely upon such oracles even today; without them the Dalai Lama may never have made it to India. Harriet Tubman, the hero of the Underground Railroad, attributed her success to messages and visions from God as to what roads to take when leading slaves to freedom.[1]

Of course, occultists don't rely only on divination for their information. Cunning Sorcerers are adept at keeping their ears to the ground and gathering information in less magickal ways as well. Marie Laveau, the Queen of New Orleans Voodoo, used information she overheard in her role as a hairdresser to help her gain access and leverage in New Orleans society. The French Sorceress and midwife La Voisin used information she gathered from her clients to influence events in the court of Louis the XIV. Count Cagliostro did the same in the court of Louis the XVI, many years later. Reading body language, engaging in skilled eavesdropping, cold reading, and gathering information from well-placed informants may not be thought of as magick, but as you will see in the chapters ahead, success is made by the interaction of magickal and mundane methods, not magickal methods alone.

Before we can plan any type of magick to influence events, be it for money, love, power, or peace, we need to gain as much information as possible about the people and places involved, so that we can attempt to find the best ways to apply our art. Whether your information is gathered by mundane or magickal means doesn't really matter, unless you are trying to impress a skeptic or appear on a television show. Most successful diviners take mundane information and use that to flesh out their divinations, which, in turn, are used to flesh out mundane knowledge. The less you separate your magickal activities from the rest of your actions, the more success you will have overall.

The exception to this rule is when you are giving a reading to a client, especially professionally. Cold reading masquerading as divination is prestidigitation, not Sorcery. If someone is paying you for a psychic reading, make sure that you are giving them the real thing, not a cold reading or an educated guess. When reading for yourself, however, information is information, whatever its source.

INTEL AND EVALUATION

There is more to intelligence gathering than just gathering the information. Information must be evaluated properly, within the context of a given situation. Intelligence agencies, for instance, differentiate between *intel* and *data*. Intel is information that has been evaluated more for its relevancy to active situations than its accuracy. Data, on the other hand, is seen as particular units of verifiable information, regardless of its current application. Whenever we receive information from any source, be it rumors at work or a tarot reading, it is vital to evaluate it for its relevancy and accuracy. In serious situations several types of divination from different sources should be consulted in order to get a full picture. If an effort can be made to verify the information by non-magickal methods, then all the better.

Intelligence agencies classify their sources into different categories: human intelligence, open source intelligence, technical intelligence, signal intelligence, measurement and signature intelligence,

financial intelligence, and so on. In the pages ahead, we will be learning how to classify the different methods of intelligence gathering
available to Sorcerers, and how each can support the other. It is a
good idea to do this with all the sources of information in your life.
What television shows do you watch? What newspapers do you read?
What books? How are they slanted? Is there counterbalance? It is all
too easy to accept information that confirms your desires and beliefs,
rather than challenges them, be it a good card reading or a partisan
talk-radio show. We all gather information all the time; it's how we
assess it and use it that's important.

The skilled Sorcerer has the capacity to be a one-man intelligence agency. Obviously, many sources of information used by the
CIA or NSA are not available to most of us reading this. Few of us
have access to spy satellites and wiretaps, but as practitioners of the
occult we do have access to divination, which thankfully comes in
many different packages. Just as the intelligence agencies use different types of intel to put together a clear picture, we must learn to use
different types of divination to complement and enhance each other.

The noted psychologist Julian Jaynes, in his book *The Origin of
Consciousness in the Breakdown of the Bicameral Mind*, categorized
divination into four categories:

1. Omens

2. Augury

3. Sortilege

4. Spontaneous divination

Sortilege is the kind most commonly used when offering readings. It includes: tarot cards, playing cards, Ifá, runes, I Ching, Mo
dice, geomancy, and any type of reading that involves the casting
of any kinds of lots. Though most books focus on mastering one or
more systems of sortilege, the successful Sorcerer will not rely just on

sortilege, but will incorporate all four types of divination into his or her intelligence-gathering activities.

Let's take a look at these four categories of divination, as well as two more advanced methods of magickal information gathering, in an attempt to put together a well-rounded strategy that can be molded to fit any situation.

OMENS

Omens are defined simply as the interpretation of unusual or important events. Lists of traditional omens are extensive and every culture has its own omens that it observes. Black cats, broken mirrors, and comets foretell bad luck. Birds flying into windows and the baying of dogs are sometimes said to foretell a death to come soon. Mockingbirds flying over the house foretells a marriage; a cat sneezing on the bride foretells it will be a happy union; a bat in the church foretells a sour divorce. Lists of traditional omens are extensive, but they are a bit limited for our purposes. The Sorcerer is no slave to superstition.

If you have been doing your regular practice of meditation, invocation, offerings, and energy working, as outlined in the first part of this book, you will soon notice that the universe seems to respond to you differently than it did before. One example of this is that certain events that, for an ordinary person, might pass unnoticed will seem to stand out as important to you. It could be a word that gets repeated over and over again by different people throughout the day, a song that you don't hear very often popping up several times on the radio, the presence of certain animals in places you would not normally see them, or a particular shape in the landscape that stands out in your psychic vision against the backdrop of normal reality. The possibilities are endless and unique to each situation. It is especially important to pay attention to omens after a ritual or spirit communication session. Often spirits that can't communicate directly will try to make themselves known through omens.

Once an omen has been spotted, you need to interpret it for it to be meaningful. Sometimes the meaning will be obvious. Often, however, you will need to seek out guidance from other types of divination. A tarot or pendulum reading can sometimes shed some light on an omen, but, more often than not, the best place to look for interpretation is other people. Sometimes we are too close to a situation to really get a clear picture of it, and one of the "intelligence assets" that any Sorcerer should cultivate is a network of other people who are gifted at divination and who can offer their wisdom when you can't see what is right in front of you.

AUGURY

Augury is a type of divination that ranks probabilities and interprets the results. The main difference between augury and omen reading is that augury is an activity you engage in consciously when you want to perform a divination, whereas omens are events that happen to you spontaneously. One of the oldest types of augury is the famous reading of entrails that was popular from Babylonian through Roman times. Basically, a sheep or lamb would be ritually cut open and the liver, which was believed by the Babylonians to be the source of blood and seat of the soul, would be examined. A healthy liver indicated good omens; a diseased organ or misshapen images within the liver would indicate a bad result. Manuals on the signs that could appear in the liver and entrails were very popular all the way through Roman times. I once tried to get a job with the Psychic Friends Network doing liver and entrails reading, but they didn't want me. Go figure.

Users of candle magick often employ augury to see how a spell will turn out by reading the wax from a candle in the spell. Candles that go out by themselves or are hard to light indicate that a spell might not work at all. A candle that burns down one side and not the other may indicate a one-sided result. Candles that produce a lot of smoke might indicate that a spell will accomplish its goal, but have unintended side effects. Even the pools of melted wax that form at the bottom of the candle are able to be interpreted by skilled augurs who can detect prophetic images within them.

More popular and widespread forms of augury include tea leaf reading, pendulums, and, of course, dowsing. Dowsing is a form of rhabdomancy, or divination with sticks, and is one of the easiest and most useful methods of augury. I highly recommend every Sorcerer at least attempt it. Old-school dowsers, especially water dowsers, will use a forked stick, but most modern dowsers use metal rods bent into an L shape. You can make your own out of a wire hanger, or purchase a premade set.

To start dowsing, simply hold one rod loosely in each hand, so that they extend straight out in front of you, and offer a prayer to bless the operation. Next "tune" your instrument by commanding the rods to cross each other. When they do, tell the rods that you want this to be the "yes" indication. Tell the rods to move apart and move to a position pointing away to the sides at about forty-five degree angles. Tell them that this is the "no" position.

Once your rods are programmed, you can use them to answer questions, to find objects, or to trace certain types of energies. First, you should tell the rods, out loud, what it is you want them to do, and ask if it is in their power to do so. The rods may actually tell you no for different reasons, in which case you can either go ahead anyway and try your luck, or switch to a different mode of divination. The reasons for a negative indication may range from your own lack of ability to perform the operation to warning you of a dangerous outcome. If they answer affirmative, you can begin your dowsing. If you are asking questions, you can simply use the yes and no positions listed above. If you are looking for an object, you can alternate between asking questions and having the rods point in the direction of the object. You can also pass them over a map and command them to cross when they are over the desired location. To use dowsing in the context of healing, pass the rods over a patient to divine the source of psychic imbalance. You can move through a haunted or disturbed area and seek the source of geopathic energies and hostile spirits in a similar fashion.

Dowsing, and all types of augury, rely upon a connection between the conscious mind, the deep mind, and the divine. As with all the other magick in this book, success depends upon the degree of your innate gift, multiplied by the effort spent in developing that gift.

SORTILEGE

A few years ago, I gave a class on tarot at a New Age store. Before I got into the cards, I passed out bags of Skittles. Everyone was told to think of a question and draw a pentagram on a piece of paper, then cast a handful of Skittles onto the pentagram. I then walked around and interpreted their charts based upon the amount of each color that appeared. For instance, one person, who asked about a job change, had a lot of red skittles in the earth section of his pentagram, indicating rapid movement in his financial sphere. But he also had a lot of purple skittles in his air section, which I interpreted as dissatisfaction with the new position's opportunities for intellectual stimulation. This went on, and several people commented that their divination seemed right on. One person even wrote me a week later to tell me that the prediction he got from the Skittles that night was more accurate than the one he got from the tarot!

The point of the exercise was to show that divination need not be couched in arcane methods, whose origins are lost to history. Indeed, many popular divination systems have developed into children's games and vice versa. Most of these fall under the umbrella of sortilege, which covers the casting of lots of all kinds and includes bones, runes, dice, shells, and, of course, cartomancy.

The Bible is filled with examples of sortilege. In the First Book of Samuel, God commands that the Jews choose a king by casting lots, which is how Saul becomes King of Israel. Elsewhere, the casting of lots is used to determine guilt, such as in the Book of Jonah, where they indicate that Jonah is the reason for the terrible storm. Jonah, of course, gets thrown overboard and winds up inside a whale, which should indicate the seriousness with which divination was approached in ancient times. Urim and Thummim were the names of lots cast in the Old Testament that are believed to come from the Hoshen, the high priest's breastplate. Though no one knows exactly how Urim and Thummim worked, the spiritual novelist Paulo Coelho, in his novel *The Alchemist*, describes them as white and black stones that are held in a bag—the black indicates "yes," the white "no." I use Coelho's interpretation myself with good results.

In Tibet, rectangular dice are frequently used in divination, called Mo in Tibetan. Before they can be read, the diviner usually undertakes a solitary retreat of several months and recites the mantra of Manjushri, the bodhisattva of intelligence, several thousand times until he receives signs of receiving the siddhi (power) of divining the future. Anyone can roll the dice and look up what they mean in a book, but in Nepal, I met properly trained Mo lamas, who underwent the traditional retreats. They gave the most amazing readings I have ever had in my life, with details that could never be guessed at, including naming specific people. Similar dice are used in the Western systems of geomancy.

I Ching and Ifá are possibly the oldest systems of sortilege on the planet, each dating back almost 5,000 years. These methods are very popular in Asia and Africa, respectively, as well as within their related diasporas. In the West, the most common form of sortilege one is likely to come into contact with is cartomancy, particularly tarot.

Now, a full treatise on tarot is, of course, beyond the scope of this book, but I thought it might be helpful to share just a few tips that I have picked up throughout the years. The first thing to know is that all the books that claim modern playing cards developed out of tarot are wrong. It may make the tarot seem more mystical, but in fact the opposite is true. Fifty-two- and fifty-six-card decks were in use for gaming and gambling hundreds of years before tarot cards were developed. So the minor arcana, at least, developed from a game, not the other way around. Paul Huson in his book *Mystical Origins of the Tarot*, the best book on tarot, bar none, in my opinion, makes a convincing argument that the major arcana developed out of medieval Christian mystery plays, while the meanings of the minor arcana cards were drawn from the Picatrix, the famous grimoires of astrological magick, and applied to playing cards.

I bring this up because as tarot develops, there are invariably purists of different stripes that make claims to the "correct" interpretation of the cards and trace it back to Egyptian, Kabbalistic, or even Atlantean sources. The truth is that the tarot went through major changes over its relatively short history of a few hundred years. Older tarot readers such as Etteilla and Comte de Mellet had in some cases radically different interpretations of the cards than did Eliphas Levi and Arthur Edward Waite, who relied on the Kabbalah rather than cartomantic tradition to supply their meanings. MacGregor Mathers, the primary force behind the Hermetic Order of the Golden Dawn, was even in conflict with himself in some cases; in his book *The Tarot*, he relies more upon tradition, which is sometimes in conflict with the meanings he supplied in the Golden Dawn papers. Skilled tarot-mancers will become familiar with meanings from multiple sources, as well as those that may be specific to the deck that they use, then use all this information as the platform from which their intuition and imagination will leap in the effort of interpretation.

Just as we learned to program the dowsing rods before performing augury, it is also important to warm up the deck before giving a reading. Through the years, I have learned dozens of ways to do this, and because I think this is one of the most neglected aspects of a reading, I want to teach you my method:

INOMINANDUM'S TAROT RITUAL

Step One: Clear the deck. Shuffle the cards while maintaining a clear mind with no thought of the reading that is to come. This effectively clears the deck of remaining patterns that would have emerged from the last reading it gave.

Step Two: Invoke. Hold the deck in the left hand and place the right hand over it in a gesture of invocation. The powers that you choose to invoke are up to you. Here is what I use:

> In the name of IAO, I invoke thee, HERMES,
> Who knows all things between Heaven and Hades.
> O Master of the magick of mercury,
> Lay your hand upon these cards,
> Consecrate them,
> Make them reveal truly the mysteries of time
> > and possibility.
> Amen.

Step Three: Programming. Keeping the deck in the same position as it was in your invocation, close your eyes and imagine that you are walking up a hill toward a cliff's edge. The Fool is at that edge appearing exactly as he does in the deck that you are using. Walk up to him and tell him the question that you want answered or the name of the person you are reading for. Also tell him the type of layout you will be using—this is most important if you use multiple layouts. Turn and walk away from the cliff, then open your eyes, shuffle until you feel that the deck has been shuffled properly, and begin your reading. As the zero card in the deck, The Fool has the ability to transmit messages to all the other genii of the deck, just as the winged helmet and sandals of the god Mercury enable him to move between worlds. The three steps of this method effectively invoke the spirit of Mercury in the macrocosm and channel it into the microcosm of the deck that you are using. If you read with playing cards instead of tarot, you can use the Joker instead of The Fool to do the same programming exercise.

As I mentioned before, most of the major methods of sortilege are too complex to do justice to in a simple chapter like this. The important thing is to become familiar with at least two methods of sortilege: one simple like geomancy or coin flipping, and one complex, like tarot, runes, or Ifá. This way you have an easy and quick method on hand for yes-or-no questions that can be used on the run, as well as a method that can reveal more complex patterns and probabilities.

SPONTANEOUS DIVINATION

Dr. Jaynes's final classification is spontaneous divination and covers quite a lot of ground. It is, at its heart, the interpretation of whatever is in front of you. Reading the Akashic records, aura reading, psychometry, and other types of direct psychic intuition are covered by this classification. These are largely gifts of the spirit, but can be developed by meditation, invocation, and the other practices discussed in the first part of this book.

Although it could easily be considered a type of augury, Jaynes includes bibliomancy under this heading. One asks a question, opens a holy book, looks for a random passage, and interprets it. The term "bible" refers not only to the Christian Bible, but to any book. Hindus have used the Vedas, Muslims the Koran and Hafiz, Romans have used Virgil, Greeks have used Homer, and so on. In fact, the practice of Sortes Homericae (a system of lots utilizing the works by Homer) was used by Socrates when he was in prison to determine on what day he would die. In his case, he drew *Iliad* 9.363: *"I shall arrive without delay at fertile Phthia, right on the third day."* Sure enough, on the third day in prison he was killed.

Early Christians, often lacking access to printed scriptures, would engage in Sortes Sanctorum (lots by saints) by listening to a sermon and waiting for words to jump out at them. Saint Augustine, for instance, is said to have converted to Christianity from Manicheanism upon hearing the words *tolle lege*, which mean "take up and read." Obviously, this is a very unreliable method of divination to all but the most adept meditators who can discern a magickally charged statement from something that simply confirms their own desires or fears.

Modern equivalents to bibliomancy are often performed with televisions and computers. Years ago, upon agreeing to start up Thelesis Camp in Philadelphia, we did a bit of televisiomancy. We asked where this project would end up, held the channel button down for several seconds, then let go when we felt the time was right. On the screen appeared a close-up of a Pennsylvania license plate followed by the car driving off into mountains in the distance. We took this to mean that the group would be firmly rooted in the area and that it would serve as a springboard for its members to travel onward. Indeed, the group, a full Lodge of the Ordo Templi Orientis, still exists in Philadelphia thirteen years later, but most of its original members have moved on to bigger and better things.

"Dreaming true" would also fall under the category of spontaneous divination. Many traditional cultures identify future Shamans or priests by a child's gift of dreaming true. In Tibet, yogis sleep with a blade of kusha grass under their pillow and body to help induce prophetic dreams. In Europe, Witches would make pillows stuffed with mugwort to aid their dreaming. The Greek Magickal Papyri give several rituals for dream divinations; most of them involve lighting a special lamp during sleep.

The images one can look for in dreams are infinitely variable and personal, well beyond what any supposed "dream dictionary" chooses to list. You can, however, ask for the images to be narrowed down for you. One of the simplest rites for a yes-or-no question to be answered in a dream is an invocation over an oil lamp before going to bed, taken from PGM VII 250-54.

> NAIENCHRE NAIENCHRE, mother of fire and water,
> you are the one who rises before ARCHENTECHTHA;
> reveal to me concerning (NN) matter. If yes, show me
> a plant and water, but if no, fire and iron. Immediately;
> quickly . . .

Another invocation from the same scroll goes almost exactly the same, but invokes Osiris and the Archangel Michael, showing how eclectic Hellenic mages and early Christians could be in their practice:

> Hail, Lord, lamp, you who shine beside OSIRIS and shine
> beside OSIRCHENTECHTHA and my lord the Arch-
> angel MICHAEL. If it is advantageous for me to do this,
> show me a plant and water, but if not, fire and iron, imme-
> diately, immediately . . .

These four classes of divination cover most of the classical methods that one would find amongst professional readers and laypeople alike. There are, however, other more advanced methods of magickal intelligence gathering that are particularly suited to the skills of a Sorcerer: viewing and interrogation.

VIEWING

Just as the NSA and CIA have their spy satellites and wiretapping, the skilled Sorcerer also has methods of observing events at a distance. In fact, in the last fifty years or so, intelligence agencies all over the world have invested significant money and time into psychic/ magickal methods of remote viewing. In 1972, the CIA invested in the Stanford Research Institute's program, which attempted to gather intelligence about psychic-spying projects in Russia and China, as well as to develop a "stable" of reliable psychics in the United States. In time, various other projects sponsored by naval intelligence and the Air Force began to spring up, all with fairly impressive results. The documents of many of these early projects became declassified in 1995, and though these programs were eventually discontinued, they seem to have produced some remarkable results, from being able to describe equipment in foreign bases, to locating hidden submarines in the Pacific within a few miles of their location.

Even the famous skeptic Richard Wiseman, a psychologist and fellow of the Committee for Skeptical Inquiry, has admitted that remote viewing has been proven using the normal standards of science. He feels, however, that an even higher standard of evidence must be provided for evaluating the "paranormal." He stated:

> I agree that by the standards of any other area of science that remote viewing is proven, but begs the question: do we need higher standards of evidence when we study the paranormal? I think we do. Because remote viewing is such an outlandish claim that will revolutionize the world, we need overwhelming evidence before we draw any conclusions. Right now we don't have that evidence. (*Daily Mail,* January 28, 2008)

Apparently even skepticism can be a matter of blind faith if we must insist on standards of evidence *higher* than what science currently provides. So much for the impartial inquiry of the scientist!

Of course, to occultists, there is nothing new about the practice of viewing distant, future, or even extra-planar events in the mind's eye or upon a special surface. This practice, commonly called scrying, has a long pedigree and many variations in its performance. Though some seers are able to simply close their eyes, direct their mind toward what they wish to see, and allow visions to appear in the darkness, most scrying is done using a focus like a scrying mirror, bowl of water, or the ubiquitous crystal ball.

Famous examples of these devices exist in legend or actuality all over the world. Persian mythology tells of the Cup of Jamshid, which was filled with the elixir of life and could reveal in its reflective surface all seven heavens. The famous Elizabethan magus John Dee used both a black Aztec mirror and a crystal globe to communicate with the angels. Both can be viewed at the British Museum in London. Seer stones played a major role in the origin of the Mormon faith, and one of Joseph Smith's stones is still held by the church to this day. In fact, before he started the Church of Latter Day Saints, he made a living by using his stones for finding buried treasure. He would place the stone in a hat and then place his face as close to the brim as possible to shroud the stone in darkness that would produce visions of where he could dig. Even US presidents have had experiences with scrying; Abraham Lincoln, according to a story in *Harper's New Monthly Magazine* issued three months after his assassination, saw a double vision of himself one evening while gazing into a mirror. One image was normal, the other pale and ghostly, which his wife took to mean that he would be re-elected, but would die in office.

The device you use in scrying, if you use any, matters little. Despite what one may infer from the popularity of crystals and mirrors in this practice, the surface need not even be particularly reflective. Lama Dawa Rinpoche, the most accurate seer I have ever met, uses a fairly dull copper disk called a melong and barely glances at it before issuing his predictions. Indian sadhus, who don't like to carry a lot of belongings during wanderings, commonly use their thumbnail for scrying. Aleister Crowley used a sapphire ring when scrying the Enochian Aethyrs. I myself alternate between a crystal ball and concave scrying mirror.

To make a proper scrying mirror, you should purchase a concave piece of glass from a company that makes or repairs grandfather clocks and paint the convex side flat black. Many magicians, including Donald Tyson and Franz Bardon, have taken a cue from

Paschal Beverly Randolph and paint the back of their mirror using a fluid condenser—a material base that conducts magickal energy. The exact recipe for the fluid condenser used by Randolph is lost to time. We only know that it included the combined sexual fluids of him and his wife mixed with psychoactive chemicals such as hashish, poppy sap, and even lettuce sap, which contains small amounts of opium. The condenser I use most is base oil that has wormwood, star anise, and mugwort soaked in it, as well as the other more personal ingredients Randolph used.

The trick to scrying is not to expect the images to appear on the surface of whatever you are using in the same manner as physical objects appear to the eye. The scrying device is there to fascinate the vision and move your mind away from the physical world. You must look into the crystal as if you are trying to see *through* it, not as if you are watching television. When the mirror starts to seem to grow in size, or the crystal seems deeper than possible, you will know that you are on the right track. Watch the periphery—visions will not appear directly at first. You must allow the *mind* to focus upon them, not the eyes. The exercises in magickal vision from the first part of the book will all come in handy here.

As to how you direct what you see in the mirror, simply state beforehand what you wish to view. Let your own deep mind and connection with the divine do the rest of the work. This is an area that is best kept as simple as possible; the more you "try," the less you will accomplish. At first I recommend just looking without any thought as to what you see—this will free you from the "lust of result" that can interfere in the early stages of learning a new technique. Once you can see images and keep them stable, work with others to set up tests, such as having someone place a simple image on a mantle or altar, then scrying to see what it is. Zener cards used in ESP tests are perfect for this, as they give a very clear and basic image to focus on.

THE WATCHER

Another method of magickal viewing is the sending of the watcher. This practice involves creating a "fetch" or "bud-will" made from your own astral essence and sending it to observe a person or place. This is similar to the creation of artificial spirits that I spoke about in *Protection and Reversal Magick,* but rather than creating a being out of elemental energy, we are simply exteriorizing a portion of our own astral essence. To accomplish this, sit comfortably with your back straight and focus your mind upon your solar plexus, which will direct the winds in the body to gather. Take several deep vase breaths and feel the accumulation of energies at that point. Once you are tuned in to those energies, exhale forcefully and will a portion of the energy and awareness from your own body to shoot out in front of you in a straight flow and gather into a sphere in front of you connected by a cord. Notice I did not say *visualize* this. Visualization can be used in this process, but if you focus too much on the particulars of the visualization you can lose the feel of it. Remember that visualization is a tool to get something to happen, not an end unto itself.

Once the sphere is created, simply instruct it to go and observe someplace or someone until you call it back. When you are ready, call the sphere back in front of you, then see its form dissipate back into the cord, which then retracts into your body. Now meditate and allow any images or impressions that have been gathered by the watcher to appear to you. Some will see very clear images this way. Some people will hear more than they see. Some will neither hear nor see, but rather feel an empathetic impression. It all depends upon your gifts and training.

This practice should be attempted only by those who have a firm grasp on protective magick and have the capacity to banish and exorcise effectively. It is vital that you recall the watcher on the same day that you dispatch it. Under **no circumstances** should you ever go to sleep without recalling the watcher. The watcher is a part of you and would be susceptible to influence and attacks of many kinds if it were connected to a dreaming host.

INFORMANTS

Even with all the types of high-tech surveillance available today, the keystone to any intelligence agency is human intelligence: people who will provide details and context that other types of intelligence leave out. In fact, the main job of the foreign intelligence agent is to develop assets, people who will provide just this type of information. Just like the foreign operative, the successful magician will develop assets that can provide information that sortilege, augury, and scrying just cannot. In the case of the occultist, we are talking about questioning not only human beings, but also spirits.

There are many types of spirits that get consulted in all corners of the globe: djinn, archangels, Loa, demons, gods, goddesses, as well as nature spirits and shades of the dead, to name just a few. The methods for contacting them are just as varied as the types of spirits themselves and range from simple séances to very complex ceremonies that can take hours. Every culture has its own protocol for contacting its spirits, and you should do a good bit of research and investigation before attempting to contact any spirits that you are not sure how to approach. Even if you are comfortable in one system of magick, such as that of the Golden Dawn, you should not assume that all spirits will respond to the same correspondences. In my book *Protection and Reversal Magick*, I told the story of a man that almost ruined his life by invoking the Orishas Yemeja and Oya into the same circle using a Golden Dawn ritual structure. The elemental attributions made sense, but he was not aware that these spirits have great enmity between them and are never served together in the same space.

If you have been practicing the daily offering ritual from Part One, then you may have already contacted, or been contacted by, local spirits. Simply calling these beings to appear and answer questions at the time of offering is a great way to work with them. In some cases, they may even contact you with unsolicited messages or warnings; such is the bond that can be created between the Sorcerer and the spirit world through the practice of offering.

A more formal spirit summoning and interrogation can be attempted with spirits that are specifically suited to providing information. Grimoires such as the Goetia and Clavicula Salomonis as well as more modern books such as Franz Bardon's *The Practice of Magical Evocation* will list spirits that can be asked all manner of questions. Because the planet that rules the mantic arts is Mercury, I often call upon Tiriel, the intelligence of Mercury.

Though after a few practices you can call upon Tiriel at any time, it is best at first if you can call upon him during the hour and day of Mercury. As with our human relationships, we must sometimes start things off formally and during appointed "office hours." Eventually, as the relationship builds, you can reach Tiriel any time using very informal methods such as visualizing his seal and chanting his name. Traditionally the day of Mercury is Wednesday. The hour of Mercury can be reckoned by two different methods. One method simply states that an hour of Mercury is in effect whenever the planet is overhead. In this case, consulting an astronomical website or chart can help determine the proper time. Another method of determining the hour is to consult the list of planetary hours that is provided below.

The trick is that these hours do not correspond exactly to the hours on the clock. The daylight hours start with sunrise, the night with sunset. To figure out the length of the hour, you must divide the time between sunset and sunrise by twelve, then figure out when on the clock your planetary time is. The good news is that there are now plenty of online planetary hour calculators that will do all the math for you. Just punch in your location and date.

Planetary Hours - Sunrise

Hour	Sunday	Monday	Tuesday	Wednesday	Thursday	Friday	Saturday
1	Sun	Moon	Mars	Mercury	Jupiter	Venus	Saturn
2	Venus	Saturn	Sun	Moon	Mars	Mercury	Jupiter
3	Mercury	Jupiter	Venus	Saturn	Sun	Moon	Mars
4	Moon	Mars	Mercury	Jupiter	Venus	Saturn	Sun
5	Saturn	Sun	Moon	Mars	Mercury	Jupiter	Venus
6	Jupiter	Venus	Saturn	Sun	Moon	Mars	Mercury
7	Mars	Mercury	Jupiter	Venus	Saturn	Sun	Moon
8	Sun	Moon	Mars	Mercury	Jupiter	Venus	Saturn
9	Venus	Saturn	Sun	Moon	Mars	Mercury	Jupiter
10	Mercury	Jupiter	Venus	Saturn	Sun	Moon	Mars
11	Moon	Mars	Mercury	Jupiter	Venus	Saturn	Sun
12	Saturn	Sun	Moon	Mars	Mercury	Jupiter	Venus

Planetary Hours - Sunset

Hour	Sunday	Monday	Tuesday	Wednesday	Thursday	Friday	Saturday
1	Jupiter	Venus	Saturn	Sun	Moon	Mars	Mercury
2	Mars	Mercury	Jupiter	Venus	Saturn	Sun	Moon
3	Sun	Moon	Mars	Mercury	Jupiter	Venus	Saturn
4	Venus	Saturn	Sun	Moon	Mars	Mercury	Jupiter
5	Mercury	Jupiter	Venus	Saturn	Sun	Moon	Mars
6	Moon	Mars	Mercury	Jupiter	Venus	Saturn	Sun
7	Saturn	Sun	Moon	Mars	Mercury	Jupiter	Venus
8	Jupiter	Venus	Saturn	Sun	Moon	Mars	Mercury
9	Mars	Mercury	Jupiter	Venus	Saturn	Sun	Moon
10	Sun	Moon	Mars	Mercury	Jupiter	Venus	Saturn
11	Venus	Saturn	Sun	Moon	Mars	Mercury	Jupiter
12	Mercury	Jupiter	Venus	Saturn	Sun	Moon	Mars

8	58	59	5	4	62	63	1
49	15	14	52	53	11	10	56
41	23	22	44	45	19	18	48
32	34	35	29	28	38	39	25
40	26	27	37	36	30	31	33
17	47	46	20	21	43	42	24
9	55	54	12	13	51	50	16
64	2	3	61	60	6	7	57

Octogram

Seal of Mercury

Seal of Tiriel

Once you have determined the proper day and time, you should draw out the seal of Tiriel on one side of a piece of parchment, and the Kamea of Mercury on the other. Attach a string or chain to the parchment so that it can be worn on your chest. If you plan on evoking Tiriel often, you can have these seals engraved upon a brass disk and kept in an orange cloth.

On the altar should be the seal of Mercury surrounded by the seals of the Royal Stars. Upon the seal, you can place the scrying device of your choice such as a crystal ball or mirror. Alternately you can place an incense burner with appropriate incense in the center of the seal.

A circle or very elaborate setup is not necessary, but if you have the room and feel like adding a bit of "oomph" to your working you can lay out an octogram on the floor. You can also add eight orange candles to the altar and any other mercurial decorations that you desire. I once led a group evocation of Tiriel where we made the octogram on the floor with Day-Glo orange tape and drew all the seals on Day-Glo orange paper. We lit the chamber with a black light and it created quite a striking, if not a bit retro-psychedelic effect. The whole idea is that you are making a sacred space that is appropriate to the entity being summoned, which in turn makes the spirit at ease and facilitates communication. It would be like you visiting another planet where they prepared a room filled with an earthlike atmosphere so that you would be comfortable and able to converse.

Once you have the time and place properly prepared you can call up Tiriel with the following invocation:

> By the powers of IAO, awesome, invisible, and ineffable;
> I call upon thee, TIRIEL, the intelligence of Mercury.
> Descend from thy celestial abode
> and appear on the throne that has been prepared
>   for thee.
> By ABLANATHANALBA, appear before me
> and answer truly all questions put to thee.
> By the power of the LOGOS
> appear without hesitation in this very hour.

If Tiriel does not show signs of appearing, either visually, audibly, or by other signs, continue to repeat his name over and over again. This strengthens the connection between you and the spirit. Often failure in this type of evocation is interpreted as a spirit not showing up, but is actually a case of the magician not being able to perceive the spirit. Use your gazes and meditate to clear the mind so that he can communicate with you.

If, after a significant effort has been made to communicate with Tiriel, he still does not appear, give the license to depart below, and pay attention to any dreams or omens that appear in the days ahead. Tiriel can utilize different methods to communicate with people of different capacity and gifts.

If Tiriel does appear, ask your questions with respect. Be humble, but be frank. Tiriel is a higher being and is not in need of any specific offerings in exchange for his services. At the end of the session, give the license to depart and close the temple:

> Thank thee, TIRIEL, for appearing when called and answering the questions put to thee. As thou came in power, so go in peace.

When thinking about informative assets, don't forget to rely upon human informants as well as spiritual ones. I mentioned the examples of Marie Laveau, Cagliostro, and La Voisin at the beginning of this chapter as magicians who cultivated human informants. No, it's not magick per se, but success in magick depends upon working the magickal *and* the mundane aspects of every situation. In the next chapter, you will learn many techniques of influencing the minds of other people that will be helpful in getting information out of people, but in general, friendly relationships with people in the right places coupled with an eye for body language and subtleties of speech can yield an amazing amount of useful knowledge. Human contacts can yield just as much useful intel as our spiritual ones, and the wise mage knows how to use both.

THE STRATEGY IN SUMMARY

The point of this chapter and the chapters that follow is to provide a comprehensive strategy rather than just a list of spells and rituals. A lot of people get card readings or have their palm read, but often this provides just a little piece of data that is fully understood only after the events have come to pass. If it was a good reading, you can look back in amazement at the accuracy of the reader, but it's rare that a single reading changes someone's course of action.

The Greeks told of a woman named Cassandra that Apollo fell in love with and gifted with the power of prophecy. When she didn't return his love, he cursed her so that no one would believe her predictions. She predicted the fall of Troy, but was powerless to stop it because no one believed her. In our case, one divination is not usually reliable enough to base life-changing action upon. Unless you are an absolute master, divinations can be wrong, misleading, or vague. This makes us a bit like Cassandra: we may get a reading indicating that something is going to happen, but are not sure enough of that reading to make the necessary changes to stop it. This is why we must develop a real strategy of intelligence gathering rather than just learning to read cards or cast runes. If multiple types of readings from multiple sources all point to the same conclusion, it's a much better bet.

By keeping an eye out for omens and synchronicities, we can pick up on approaching important events and pivotal moments. By utilizing sortilege, augury, and spontaneous divination on a regular basis we can actively monitor the future for anything of interest. Keeping a diary of divinations is very useful for tracking your accuracy and improving your performance.

If we do have a particular problem or interest that arises, we need to apply not just one reading, but multiple readings from different systems to arrive at what we can call *actionable intelligence*. A tarot reading can be confirmed by a dowsing session, which in turn can be explored further with dream divining. In important situations, we can consult Tiriel or a similar spirit to illuminate our situation.

It is always a good idea to back up your divinations with input from other readers. Every serious occultist that I know has at least two close friends that they can consult for readings. This is especially important when the matter is deeply personal and our feelings will draw us to interpret things in the most favorable way, rather than the most likely.

If we get good information from our divinations, we can sometimes use this information to aid in questioning real people. Years ago I did a series of divinations about the company I worked for and all of them indicated that there would be big changes, but I couldn't tell if I would be laid off or not. Using the information from the divinations, I was able to get a manager to open up about the specifics of the coming changes since it seemed I already knew so much about it.

As important as divination is, we must not overdo it. I have met people that become so obsessed with divination that they will hardly leave their home without a card reading to tell them things will be okay. Divination is useful, but it is not vital to every action. If you find yourself divining several times a day, you are divination dependent and need to back off. If you have been practicing the daily practices taught in the first part of the book, you can trust in divine guidance to steer you on the right path overall. Stick to doing a monthly group of divinations to scan for trouble and go deeper only if you have a situation that really warrants it.

The last point I want to make is that the best divination is the one that *doesn't* come true. Ideally, divination should provide enough actionable intelligence to avoid or improve the prediction. Time is not linear, and the future is by no means written. Every moment consists of just one of an infinite amount of probable futures collapsing into the present. Through divination we can get a feel for these probabilities, and through Sorcery we can alter them to our benefit and the benefit of others.

NEW EDITION COMMENTARY—
THOUGHTS ON DIVINATION

This root idea of this chapter rests in the separation of data versus intelligence. Data points are the building blocks of actionable intelligence. Single divinations of any kind are a single point of data. Just like economists, political pundits, and weathermen can be wrong, even the best diviners are wrong on occasion and give only a partial picture most of the time. If the situation you are reading on is coming up fast, or doesn't have anything important at risk, a single divination is probably fine. If however you are investing your life savings or starting a risky business venture, you will want more to go on than a single divination. A lot of readers may be upset at me for saying this, but divination of any kind should be only one factor in your decision-making, and rarely a main factor. That said, I have a few key pieces of advice for anyone engaged in divination.

1. It's better to be wrong than vague: I get it, you don't want to be wrong. No one does. Unfortunately, one of the tactics that readers use to protect themselves from being wrong is not committing to any firm message at all. If you give vague generalities and esoteric fluff, then no matter what happens you can look back and interpret events in a way that lets you claim to be at least partially right. The problem is, that makes divination useless. If you are often saying, "Ah-ha! That's what that reading meant!" after events unfold, then the information wasn't very useful ahead of time.

2. Go ahead and be detailed. Be blunt, brutal even, with your predictions. Yes, you may be proven wrong, but many professionals get paid hefty sums for providing their best projections and predictions. If you are a good reader, you will be right a good amount of the time. If you aren't, then why bother with divination at all?

3. Don't second-guess the cards: In the effort not to be proven wrong, diviners will often second-guess or reinterpret their reading based on other data points. Don't do it. If your divination is clear, then stand by what it says. You can even disagree with it, saying, "The cards say X even though every other indicator says Y." Just don't let your doubt or second-guessing color your reading.

In August 2016, I did a public reading that indicated Donald Trump would win the presidential election, an outcome I did not want to believe. Still, I posted it publicly for people to see and scrutinize. In October of that year I was asked in front of a crowd of people if I still stuck by that interpretation. I said, "Look, no one thinks he is going to win. No polls show him winning, no newspapers predict him winning, and even I don't think that he will win. The *cards* however did show him winning and I am not going to change my reading just because I think it's wrong based on other types of data." Needless to say, the cards were right. Other times the cards are wrong, but if you are going to make actionable intelligence, you can't ignore or second-guess your divination.

4. You don't need to divine before every act of magick. If the first point upset a few readers, this one is surely going to upset a few magicians. I was taught to always do a reading before any spell to see how it will manifest. Sometimes I still do, but most of the time I don't. Magick is a real thing, and its actions aren't significantly different from other real things. If doing something is a good idea, then I do it. If it isn't a good idea, I don't. A divination will almost never change my mind about whether something makes sense or not.

5. Sometimes a divination would prevent someone from doing something that otherwise makes perfect sense, which might be even worse. Let's say I am excited about a job offer, and a

divination indicates that something will go wrong if I take the job: Should I not take it? When was the last time you ever did anything important and *nothing* went wrong? Every job I had, every house I have owned, every course I have taught, every woman I have dated has had a downside, but I wouldn't trade any of them.

6. By all means, divine whenever you feel like you need to, or if something feels particularly tricky, but don't become dependent upon it. Even the best readers do not see all.

CHAPTER 6

Influence and Persuasion

There is no more quintessential power of the Sorcerer than the ability to influence the mind of another. "Charmed," "enchanted," "spell-bound," "ensorcelled," and "fascinated" are all words that originally indicated someone under a spell, but have now become common expressions in English. Some of the most well-known magicians, such as Rasputin and Casanova, rose to prominence in large part due to their ability to charm powerful people through the skilled combination of magick and charisma. Although magick and charisma depend a small part on nature's gifts, the larger part of both can be learned and perfected through practice.

The magick presented in this chapter will affect all the further chapters in the book. It should be fairly obvious how the use of influence and persuasion has applications in other sorcerous pursuits. Whether seeking love, wealth, or favorable outcomes in court, influencing the minds of key players will be part of your strategy. The topic is complex enough and important enough on its own that we need to deal with it separately before incorporating it into wider magickal plans.

ETHICS OF INFLUENCE

Before getting into the technical aspects of influence, we need to deal with the ethical considerations. Although the magick of persuasion and compelling is universal, and it exists in every religion and culture on the planet, there are some modern traditions of Wicca and New Age thought that consider it taboo. The idea is that to rob the free will of another person is unethical, ergo magick aimed at influencing the will of another is also unethical. Although well-intentioned, I find this view to be a bit simpleminded and to not really reflect a good understanding of will, ethics, or magick. If this is your view, then I ask you to consider the following: *You cannot **not** influence people.*

This phrase is a key axiom in the field of neurolinguistic programming and should be kept in mind throughout your reading of this chapter: "You cannot not influence people." Everything you do, everything you wear, everything you say influences those around you. When you go to a job interview or on a first date, you probably wear your best outfit for the occasion. You stand and sit with good posture, you suck in the belly. You talk yourself up more than you normally would. Maybe you even exaggerate a little. You present yourself in an ideal fashion so that you can get your foot in the door. This is purposeful influencing. If, however, you just throw on any old thing, let it all hang out, and talk as casually as you would to your best friend, this is also influence, it's just not skilled or intentional influence. Because you are always influencing others, isn't it better to be skillful at it than not?

Some will say that the examples I give are normal influences, and that magickal influence is different. These same folks often point out to detractors that magick and Witchcraft are not supernatural, but use natural forces that mainstream society doesn't understand.

Because magick is a natural advantage, I see no reason to deem it any more unethical than wearing one's best suit. Someone's natural attractiveness or family connections are also natural advantages, not significantly different from magick in effect. Is it unethical to be well connected and good-looking?

Dion Fortune points out that over-the-top aggressive magickal influence can be considered a type of psychic attack, and I agree. But it's a matter of degree and intent that makes it an attack, not simply the influence itself. Most spells will only plant seeds in someone's mind, tilting it one way or the other, not completely dominate their will. If this were not the case, Pagan festivals and occult gatherings would be filled with supermodels hanging on the arms of unattractive, broke-ass would-be wizards, fascinated by their every arcane theory. If you have not spent much time around groups of occultists, trust me, this is not the case.

There are, of course, stronger degrees of influence than can be gotten from your average spell. The following pages will provide some of the secrets necessary to reach these degrees, but still, we will not be reaching the complete domination of the will that is often depicted in movies and books. That is not to say that such techniques don't exist within the annals of magick. They do. They usually involve prolonged brainwashing, psychoactive drugs, and an onslaught of intense magickal rituals. The zombie-making rites carried out by some secret societies in Haiti would be an example of a process that involves all of the above and more. But even here, intent is what makes it evil, not the act itself. Societies such as the Sanpwel or Bizango sometimes carry out these rituals as a way to avoid killing criminals that the law cannot touch. Zombification is, in their view, an ethical alternative to capital punishment.

Another example of extreme influence, but a little more down-to-earth, would be the various types of "do this or be cursed" spells. Here the influencing spell has the added power of tormenting or even killing the target until they comply. I have on my desk a candle called the Omnipresence of God. It is a candle that is mostly used for love. It has a rather harmless looking design of a bearded God with scales of judgment on the front, and the following Prayer to the Intranquil Spirit on the back:

"Oh, Intranquil Spirit, you that in hell are wandering and will never reach heaven, hear me. I want to get you the five senses of (name) and you should not let him rest in peace, either seated or standing or sleeping. That he should find himself as deserted as the waters of the seas. That he should run and run until he humbly falls at my feet because nobody would help him. Neither a divorcée nor a married woman, nor a widow should love him. I conjure you before the cross and God that you are to run after me as the living after the cross and the dead after the light. Amen."

I would consider this a bit too extreme a length to go to for a love spell, but clearly many people do not. Mind you, I bought the candle not at a botanica or occult store, but at the local Shop Rite!

Although some may like to jump to this kind of action, I find that unless I am trying to influence someone who is posing a physical danger to others, there are better methods of influence and persuasion that do not require curses to carry out. The degree of influence that you find ethical is up to you. All the methods presented from here on in are ones that I have found effective, but do not cross the line (at least in my opinion) into brainwashing or psychic attack.

There are two types of magickal influence: *direct* and *indirect*. Direct influence is any spell, ritual, or action aimed directly at influencing the mind of a specific individual. Indirect influence consists of spells, actions, and behavioral changes focused on you, with the intent of making you more influential in specific ways. For example: making a poppet of your boss and performing a ritual to get a raise would be direct influence, as would using gazes, hypnotic techniques, and magickally charged words in conversations with them. Anointing yourself in the morning with commanding oil, doing Jupitarian invocations, and taking extra effort in your dress, grooming, and behavior to build an aura of confidence, competence, and command would be indirect influence. Another way to look at it is outer and inner Sorcery: direct influence aims at a target other than yourself; indirect is aimed at making internal changes for yourself.

Indirect Influence

Because work on yourself is always more important and long-lasting than work done on others, we should start with indirect influence first. Also, it should be fairly obvious that developing an influential persona will be an important asset in helping along your targeted spells.

Consider the type of influence that you want to have. Do you want to be seen as a powerful businesswoman in order to shatter the glass ceiling at your job? Maybe you want to be the debonair seducer. Perhaps you need to appear as a threatening presence at a law enforcement job, or a charismatic charmer for sales. Each of these characters exudes a type of influence and command, and a skilled Sorcerer can step into any role that they will.

Talk of taking or changing personas to achieve an end makes some uncomfortable because it seems to violate the notion of "being yourself." It is as if adherence to the set of likes, dislikes, and mechanistic behavioral patterns that you have accumulated in life thus far is somehow a virtue in and of itself. Liking who you are is all well and good, but it can also be an excuse. Lazy, angry, and egotistical people always seem to use "it's just how I am" as an excuse for bad behavior. *Being yourself* is fine if you are speaking of the deepest aspects of your soul, but more often than not, it's just habits and surface level traits that we are clinging to as a "self." If we get too hung up on who we already are, we can lose sight of who we can become.

In 1904, a man named Archibald Leach was born to a poor family in Bristol, England. He had a confused and unhappy childhood, and having been thrown out of school at the age of fourteen, he came to America to remake himself. Rather than just *be himself*, he carefully studied the behaviors of successful people, adopting higher-class mannerisms and dress. He trained himself to speak in a distinctive mid-Atlantic accent and began to make inroads into Hollywood. Noting that the initials C and G had worked out well for Gary Cooper and Clark Gabel, he renamed himself Cary Grant. He would even reinforce his transformation through small magickal acts hidden in his movies. In *Arsenic and Old Lace* one of the stones in the graveyard reads "Archie Leach"; and in *His Girl Friday*, he responds to a pointed comment by saying, "The last man who said that to me was Archie Leach, just a week before he cut his throat."

Developing the Influence Self

Just as Archibald Leach turned himself into Cary Grant, so too can we turn ourselves into whoever we need to be. Begin by taking stock of yourself. Have someone take a few photos of you and make a few recordings of yourself on video. Study yourself. What accent do you speak in? Do you say "um" and "like" in almost every sentence? Do you curse a lot? Does the way you dress compliment you? What is your style? How do you hold yourself when you sit? Do you fidget? Do you smile when you walk into a room?

The next step is to study people that exemplify what you wish to achieve. Watch your boss, and your boss's boss. How do they dress? How do they act and speak? Spend some time with a friend who is smooth with the opposite sex. How does he approach people? What about his or her demeanor exudes confident sexiness? Find movies with characters who exude the qualities that you wish to convey. Read the autobiographies of famous politicians, businessmen, actors, and lovers. The trick isn't figuring out specific things that you think make the difference, the trick is trying it all out. There is nothing wrong with trying someone else's body language or speech patterns on for size. Do it even if you don't think it's important. Eventually, as you adopt and drop different behaviors, you will be able to chart their influence and can then keep what you want and drop what you don't based upon experimentation and experience.

Read a few books such as *How to Win Friends and Influence People* or *The 7 Habits of Highly Effective People*, but don't read too many of them. A few books will give you valuable keys to play with. Too many will simply weigh you down with repetitive advice and delay your actually taking action. Doing is more important than knowing. In the end you will find simple things such as spending extra time on grooming, dressing correctly for an occasion, walking into rooms smiling, remembering people's names, and treating other people better will make tremendous changes in how you are perceived, and thus your influence over others.

SOCIAL PROOF

Another simple technique to manage how you are perceived is the use of social proof modifiers. Social proof is basically the environment and people that surround you and what they say about you. A famous experiment in social proof was conducted in April 2007 when Joshua Bell, the famous violin virtuoso, played his Stradivarius in the DC Metro during rush hour as if he were just another street musician. Not surrounded by adoring fans and all the fanfare of a theater, he made only $32 and didn't make much of an impact on passersby. Although the surroundings of a struggling street musician negatively modified Bell's social proof, there are many ways to positively modify our social proof as well.

Several years back, I suffered a very dry spell romantically. Even with the help of Sorcery, I couldn't seem to generate interest from the opposite sex. I shared my problem with a female friend of mine, who suggested a course of action. She would attend an upcoming party and act like my girlfriend, then later give me space to meet other people. Though this sounded like a bit of a crazy plan at the time, I was more than willing to be seen with her on my arm, even if it was just a ruse. The plan worked. After I left her in another room, I immediately started making conversation with a woman who gave me her phone number. The dry spell was soon broken, because I was able to convey value by positive social proof.

I recently read about an even more drastic use of social proof. A student at Yale started a one-man company, with himself as CEO. He hired a service that acts as receptionist and answering service for small businesses and started handing out cards with his title as CEO. Eventually he was able to fund the cost of the answering service by selling titles to friends who were in on the scheme. They would hand the cards to girls at bars and potential employers alike. If anyone called the number on the card, they got a professional receptionist who confirmed the existence of the company and that person's position, and would then offer to direct the caller to voicemail. A bit deceptive perhaps, but certainly an ingenious way to exercise a bit of influence and persuasion. Always act like someone who already has the job/lover/position/outcome that you want, and you will be one step closer to achieving it.

INVOCATIONS

Once we determine the types of changes we desire to make in ourselves, we can start applying Sorcery to assist our efforts. Let's take the example of someone who desires advancement in a corporation. A good way to begin would be to start every day with an invocation to the powers of Jupiter, which is the planetary power that rules wealth, power, and command. You can use a classical invocation, or one of your own. I include here a ritual called "The Conjuration of the Commander," which will serve as an example.

THE CONJURATION OF THE COMMANDER

If you know where Jupiter is in the sky, you can face that direction. If not, then stand facing north with a straight back and closed eyes. Perform the centering meditation and imagine that the planet Jupiter is directly above you. It is immense: 1,000 times larger than the earth. Perform the splitting of space, then, throwing your arms upwards, see the symbol of Jupiter in blazing blue above you. Sound the Greek vowel upsilon, which is pronounced OO as in "book." The pitch should start high and end low. Seed syllables are powerful sounds that can penetrate right to the core of the force that you are invoking or projecting. In this case, you should feel that the force begins to flow from the planet toward the sigil in front of you at the high pitch, and then into your body as the pitch deepens.

After the utterance of the seed syllable, invoke the following:

Overshadowing orb of omnipotence
Magnanimous and mighty,
Supreme sphere
I utter the sacred seed sound,
And offer it in praise
Echo it back upon me with Jovian grace
Thy lightning illuminates my mindstream
Thy thunder carries the blessings of your sphere
May it take seat within my heart and mind
May it reflect outward though my hand and eye
I am the kind commander
I am the wielder of wealth
I am the holder of the scepter
I am the perfector of health
My voice thunders and inspires obedience
My eyes flash and inspire devotion

By the power of (oo)
By the grace of IAO
Grow forth and witness!

At the conclusion of the invocation, use the pore breathing technique to absorb the energies of Jupiter. See yourself growing and towering over the earth, bigger even than Jupiter itself. Reflect on the sheer immensity of the universe and the comparative smallness of your own life and problems.

Open your eyes and anoint your head, throat, chest, and hands with commanding oil or similar condition oil.

Depending upon the type of influence that you are seeking, you may want to use a Solar, Mercurial, or Venusian invocation, but for our example of the aspiring executive, this works well. You will find other invocations that fit the bill in the chapters ahead, as well as other practices aimed at creating specific auras of influence around yourself, be they for love, business, power, or wrath.

I stress again here the necessity for the magickal and mundane efforts to complement each other. The Conjuration of the Commander, performed without any real effort on your part to learn the skills of effective leadership, success, and influence, will likely not have a very strong effect. It may cast you in a slightly better light with some, but by not putting forth the real-world effort you are wasting the influence of the planet. First comes the working, then comes the work.

A good nighttime practice to accompany this work is the "Prayer of the Perfected Self," which is a personal affirmation practice combined with an invocation to a group of powers known as the Amelektoi. The idea here is that you first build up a lot of qualities that you would like yourself to have and come up with a mantra to encapsulate them. For example, the comic book writer and magician

Grant Morrison once used the phrase "I am as cool as James Bond" as a mantra.[1] Then, once you have this made clear you invoke the Amelektoi, which consist of the Iungges, Synochs, and Teletarchs. The Iungges are sometimes called the howlers and generate new patterns in the world. The Synochs are maintainers, who keep these patterns moving. The Teletarchs are the perfectors, who manifest the pattern into reality. To learn more about the Amelektoi, study the Chaldean Oracles.

THE PRAYER OF THE PERFECTED SELF

Light two candles, one white and one black. Place them two feet in front of you facing east. The black should be on your left, the white on the right. They should be either on the floor or each on a separate table, so that if you take one step forward you will be standing between them.

Light the candles and perform the centering meditation. In the temple of the mind, see the candles as great pillars. The white pillar on your right represents your desire for gnosis and enlightenment: to elevate yourself beyond your limits and unlock the divine spirit within you. The black pillar on your left represents your desire for power: for wealth, love, and material fulfillment. You stand at this moment in a time out of time. Behind you is your past, the millions upon millions of actions, chances, and factors that have brought you to the current moment. In front of you is the unknown future.

Spend a few moments contemplating how the two pillars are equally important and complementary. The light of gnosis shines outward through material action, and material action enables the aspirant to achieve greater heights of gnosis. See an image of yourself in the space between the pillars. This image of yourself is occupying a place just one step ahead of you in the future. Imagine that this being possesses all the qualities that you wish to have.

Invoke the following:

By the power of IAO
Existence of existence
All-embracing fullness
I call forth the implacables!
Iungges! Spin forth and howl forth my will
Synochs! Grow forth and make lucid my spell
Teletarchs! Make it manifest unto matter
My will is the will of the father
My wisdom is the wisdom of the mother
Revolve!
Bind!
Shine forth!
I shall be as I will to be
I am . . .

Here recite a list of qualities that you wish to possess, such as, "I am cunning. I am desirable. I am enlightened. I am kind." Recite them as much as you like. The repetition has the psychological benefit of a positive affirmation, but done in this context it is given the weight of the divine will, which is enacted by our triad of powers. Invoke the following:

Thus the fates have spun
Thus it has begun.

Step forward one step so that you are between the candles/ pillars and occupying the same space as your projected future self. Spend a couple moments in meditation, then thank the powers and close the temple.

DIRECT INFLUENCE

Direct influence is the application of skillful persuasion at a specific target. Hopefully you will have developed your indirect influence to a point that some of your work is already done, but there are times when we need specific people to do specific things, and in these cases we must take aim and let loose with all our spells and cunning.

Observing the Target

Start by studying the target. Pay attention to the things they say, but more importantly to the things they do. I would not recommend going so far as to follow them around, or you might find yourself charged with being a stalker. Simply find out as much about them as you can. Some things to look for and note:

- What type of behavior upsets them?

- How is their self-esteem?

- What activities do they enjoy outside of work?

- Can you get access to any personal items or documents of theirs?

- Do they have siblings?

- What are their "repeat phrases"?

- Are they neat or sloppy?

- Are they more analytical or emotional?

- Are they left- or right-handed?

- Are they visual, kinesthetic, or auditory thinkers?

That last one needs some explanation. There is a theory that people tend to be either kinesthetic (sense of touch), visual (sight), or auditory (hearing) in their thinking. You can tell what type people are by paying attention to how they describe things. If they tell stories of *what they heard* versus *what they saw* versus *how it made them feel* then it gives a big clue. Take the example of a project at work. You might hear someone say: *"It sounds like a good approach to me," "I feel good about it,"* or *"I can see how this is going to work already."* These three statements each would give clues as to what type of thinking the target uses.

Simply by paying attention to these clues, we can learn to communicate our ideas more directly. If someone is visually oriented and you want to suggest something to them by saying, *"How does X sound to you?"* you are not going to get as far as if you say, *"How does X look to you?"* It sounds silly, but it works. Try it out.

The previous technique of kino/visual/auditory programs is commonly used in the discipline of neurolinguistic programming or NLP. Another useful trick for the observant Sorcerer from NLP is to watch the eyes of a target to see what part of the brain they are accessing at a particular moment. For instance, people who look up and to your left are usually accessing visually constructed thought. People who look up and to your right are accessing visual memory. People who look down and to your right are usually having an internal dialogue.

How does this help us influence people? Simple: you can gauge your conversation to their thoughts. For instance, if you are trying to sell a car to someone and you are talking about the freedom that is felt by owning a convertible sports car, but the person is looking to your left, you know that they are probably crunching numbers instead of going along with your spiel and remembering that feeling. You can change your sales pitch to play down the cost of the vehicle and get into how insignificant the monthly payments would actually be. If they look straight ahead, a sign of being ready for more input, you can go back to the "feeling of freedom" angle and see how their eyes react. If they are looking down and to your right, they are accessing their memory, which is what you want. All that, and we haven't even really applied any direct influence yet, just clever observation!

Below is a handy chart to memorize. It is labeled as if you are looking right at the person, so the notations are all to *your* right and left, not the target's.

Visual constructed   Visual remembered

Auditory   Auditory
constructed   remembered

Kinesthetic   Auditory dialogue

Magickal Links

One of the things that your observation of the target should have revealed is what kind of magickal links you can get a hold of. The more personal the link, the stronger the outcome. This is something that experience has shown me is hard for people to understand. When requesting links from clients I get questions such as, "Can't you just think of the person?" or "Can't I just send you a photo?" The answer is sure, if that's all you have. It's not a very strong link to work with. Pictures are excellent to help your focus when used together with a personal link, but are surprisingly weak links in and of themselves. As for just thinking of the person, purely mental efforts in magick yield purely mental results. If you want tangible results, make tangible efforts. Go for something more personal. In the past, Sorcerers have gone to great lengths and risk to obtain hair, fingernail clippings, articles of clothing, or signed documents. I am not telling you to steal or anything like that, but if you use your imagination you can usually come up with something.

The quality of a link can be rated in two ways: *intimacy* and *relation to the work.* For instance, if you are trying to get someone to have sex with you, their business card isn't so great, but their unwashed underwear is top notch! If, however, you are trying to get a job, the business card's value just went up several notches, though a signed document is still better. Keep this in mind when getting links.

Ladder of Command

One of my favorite ways to establish a link with a person is to use a Witch's ladder to "capture their voice." This is a very simple piece of magick that requires nothing but a string, preferably of a color that corresponds to the type of influence you wish to have over them. First, cleanse the string with salt water or whiskey to remove any previous patterning. Then take the string someplace where you will be in earshot of the target, but not seen, such as in another cubicle at work or in another room at home. Tie a knot loosely in the string, but do not pull it tight yet. Call the target's name, and the exact moment they answer, pull the knot tight! Do this until there are ten knots in the string, and then once more to seal the loop with the eleventh and final knot.

Obviously you will be a bit conspicuous, not to mention annoying, if you try to get all eleven knots in one day, so break it up throughout several days. Once you have your ladder of eleven knots, you can use it in a number of ways. You can dress it with appropriate condition oil such as Compelling Oil, Love Me Oil, or Bend Over Oil. You can even wear it as a necklace or bracelet to signify that you have this person "wrapped around your finger."

SETTING TRAPS AND TRIGGERS

Another angle on magickal links is to set traps and spell triggers so that rather than taking a link of your target to the site of a spell, you are taking your spell to the target. My favorite way to do this is with powders. Though there are hundreds of kinds of condition powders (as well as corresponding oils, soaps, and incense), here we are primarily concerned with the various types of influencing blends. When browsing through a catalogue of these products, you may see similar sounding names, but each name usually indicates a different strength or purpose. Compelling powder is usually used to get people to do things they have already promised to do, such as pay money or render a service. Controlling powder is used to get people to do things that they might not normally do and is thus stronger than Compelling. Domination or Bend Over powders are even stronger than that and may be used to lead people into real submission.

You can purchase these condition products at any well-stocked occult store, or you can make them yourself. A full listing of recipes would require a book in itself and thus is beyond the scope of the present work. However, many are easy enough to make. For instance, you can use High John, calamus root, and licorice root for Domination work. Soak them in a carrier oil like almond oil to make the oil, or blend them with talcum for the powder. You can burn them as incense alone, or if you know how, you can mix them to make incense powder or sticks. I confess that I usually purchase my products, but as long as you look for a good supplier, such as the Lucky Mojo Curio Company, you won't go wrong.

When you decide on the powder that you want to use, you should pray over it fervently to activate it. This is best done with simple words of your own devising that clearly state your intent. Once the powder is charged, you can apply it in a number of ways. Keep some powder in your pocket and dust someone when you give them a handshake. You can also apply powder to a note or document that you give to them. Be sure to shake most of it off, especially if you are mailing it! It only takes a little bit to carry the effect, and the post office doesn't take kindly to powders being sent in the mail these days. More commonly you can plant powder for the target to walk upon by sprinkling some in their doorway or under their desk or even in their shoes. Sneaky Sorcerers have even been known to add the powder to a target's bottle of talcum powder, so that they end up dusting themselves! Figure out what you have access to, then do your best.

Another option is to feed a philter or even your own links, such as body hairs, to the target. While some may find it distasteful, women have been using this technique for years, putting everything from hair to various bodily fluids into their target's food.

TEMPLE SPELLS

After you set things working with your field magick, you need to back it up with some work in your temple. For instance you can use the ladder of command that you made to tie up a red figure candle and dress it all in Domination herbs to gain control over your lover for a time. Similarly, because skull candles are often used in influencing magick (representing the light of your influence entering their head) you can wrap it around a green skull candle and "massage" Bend Over oil, and thoughts of promotion, into his brain.

My favorite use for the ladder is simply to use it as a rosary. Late at night, when you think the target is asleep, light some incense appropriate to the work and hold the ladder over it as if you were actually dangling the target over the fire. Repeat your commands over and over again, counting off on each knot as you go. I find this approach to be amazingly effective, and more than a little cathartic.

You can set lights on your altar by making simple petitions and setting an appropriately dressed candle on them. For the petition, you can either write a letter describing exactly what you desire the target to do, or use a very traditional method of writing the target's name nine times in lowercase letters, then crossing it with your own name in capital letters nine times. Whereas most candles are dressed with oil pulling it either toward you or away from you, candles used in influencing magick have the oil twisted on to represent the bending of their will to your own.

GRASPING AND TRAMPLING

A whole Master Root is an excellent addition to any Sorcerer's altar. Because the root appears to have many twisted and tentacle-like appendages to place things in, it has long been associated with binding magick. Because my Sorcery altar is inside a large closet, I like to suspend my root from the ceiling by a string and place personal links and paper talismans in its folds to keep them grasped tightly, until I have need of using them in more specific spells.

For cases where it's vital that you gain and maintain the upper hand on someone, a very common and simple spell is to place a picture or object link of that person in your shoe, so that you are always walking on them. You can dress it in Bend Over oil or powder for added strength. At times when you need to really dominate the target, you can even grind your foot down or stomp hard on it. Use this one only for those with whom you have harsh adversarial relations.

CONVERSATIONAL SORCERY

I could go on and on with spells to gain influence over people, but there is more to influence than just spells. There are also cunning ways of deploying sorcerous gestures and vocal commands when your target is right in front of you. These are similar to the techniques in the chapter on subtle keys, but aimed at influencing magick.

Dropping Anchors

Anchors are an NLP term for events that your mind associates with a specific feeling or idea. The most famous example of an anchor is probably Pavlov's bell. Pavlov was a psychologist who would ring a bell before feeding his dogs every day. Eventually he could get the dogs to salivate simply by ringing the bell with no food present. People experience anchors all the time. Songs that evoke the nostalgia of old lovers and smells that remind you of mom's kitchen are examples of anchors. Your morning coffee signaling the brain that it's time to wake up even before the caffeine hits your system is another.

The anchors mentioned above are all examples of ones that have been set over long periods of time, but a skilled practitioner can set and use anchors in the course of just one conversation. Returning again to the example of a car salesmen talking about the feeling of freedom and joy that came with owning a first car, while the salesman is doing this he can make a physical gesture such as stroking his chin. If he does this a few times, later in the conversation he can stroke his chin and remind the client of this feeling of freedom and joy without ever mentioning the pitch. In courses on advanced techniques of public speaking, students are taught how to set anchors for the audience by saying different things at different points on the stage. Eventually, by moving to a particular spot on the stage, your audience will experience a certain response. This, in itself, is magick, but is taught openly in corporate marketing, sales, and speaking seminars. Just because modern society has accepted it and uses it, that doesn't mean it's not part of magick anymore. Of course, Sorcerers will be able to amplify the effects using direct application of energy, which I will get to shortly.

In a sense, most of the gestures and correspondences of magick are anchors. If a ceremonial magician uses the color red, it probably evokes feelings of martial power because of its association with the planet Mars. If a Tibetan magician sees the color red, it is associated with the magick of enchanting and influencing people. If a Rootworker sees red, it evokes the magick of sex. Colors, gestures, directions, and words are all anchors that are used to call certain powers and feelings to mind based on their prior associations that are set by tradition.

Because one thing may have different associations in different systems of magick, it is tempting to think that the correspondences have no real meaning of their own and exist only in your own mind. This is a mistaken view. Although it is true that the correspondences of color, direction, and so on have no inherent and universal meaning, that doesn't mean that they don't have a firm meaning beyond just your own brain. They have a *meaning within the current of magick that you are working*, and as long as you are standing within that current, you should take heed of their meaning. This is important to know. Although you can interface with multiple systems of magick, that doesn't mean that all the rules are just in your head and you can do whatever feels right with no consequences.

To illustrate this point I will share a story. An old roommate of mine was once making a daily practice of a Jupiter-Invoking Hexagram ritual that used the Golden Dawn style of drawing the hexagram in certain specific patterns to invoke certain planets. Instead of feeling the power of Jupiter flowing through him, however, he spiraled into a depression and uncharacteristic sluggishness for weeks. One morning, while I was watching him do his daily practice, I noted that he was making Saturn-Invoking Hexagrams by mistake. Though he didn't know the system well enough to know the difference, even subconsciously, the mistake caused Saturnian energies to be evoked. Despite his intent, despite his will, the technical mistake caused the wrong planetary energy to be invoked. Clearly, the correspondence between the gesture and the planet existed beyond just his mind.

In short, while the correspondences of a system may not have independent and universal existence, *the current that they exist within does*. If you evoke a being or power from one system by the protocols of another, if your ritual works at all, it may not take it kindly. If you choose to work with multiple currents, a perfectly natural thing to do in our increasingly small and multicultural world, you need to take this into account. That said, let's take a look at how to use all this effectively in conversation.

If we know how to channel different energies subtly, without all the show of the tools and robes that one might use in the temple, we can impregnate our anchors with magick. One way to do this is to use the pore breathing techniques from the first section of the book.

Fill your body with the essence of a pure element or planetary power, then channel it toward the gesture that you are using as an anchor. Not long ago I used this technique to calm down a family member that I knew would be upset when I had to share some bad news. I started the conversation by saying some flattering and calming things while placing my hand over my heart. Meanwhile, I quickly accumulated elemental water energy into my heart. After I broke the news and could see this person starting to fly off the handle, I dropped the anchor by placing my hand over my heart again and letting the elemental water flow between us. The combination of the psychological trigger of the anchor and the application of elemental water took this person quickly back into a calmer state, where they could rationally handle the bad news.

In the Arya Tara Kurukulla Kalpa, a magickal text associated with the goddess Kurukulla, whom we will meet at the end of the chapter, there are techniques for controlling other people by accumulating enchanting energy through seeing a silent mantra encircling the heart, then letting that energy flow out in hooked lights that enter the right nostril of the target and flow out the left nostril back into your body. I have used this technique while using traditional mudras (hand gestures) from that Tantra as anchors. The effect on the target was immediate and amazing. They were repeating everything I said and agreed to it all. I was tempted to end the conversation with "these are not the droids you're looking for,"[2] but figured that would probably blow it. . . .

Vox Magicae

Apart from anchors, there are ways to embed hidden commands in your speech by fluctuating the tone of your voice for certain words cleverly hidden inside your sentences. This technique of indirect suggestion was pioneered by the famous psychologist Milton Erickson who would often treat patients with stories that contained embedded commands. A boy brought to him with problems of bed-wetting would have a few sessions consisting of stories about baseball and the muscles used in controlling a pitch so that the ball is released at only the right time. Bed-wetting was never mentioned in the session, but the boy would be programmed by the embedded commands in the stories about muscle control.

Of course these embedded commands can be used for more than therapeutic methods. They are in fact used on you all the time in commercials and media. Sometimes they are even used unintentionally. Because the deep mind does not interpret negative suggestions well, often when we are told not to do something, our deep mind instantly desires to do just that!

You can use embedded commands to program people as well. All you need to do is place your command within a sentence and say the command words in a different tone or pitch than the rest of the sentence. An easy way to do this is to change the palate resonance of your words. When you speak, you feel a vibration in your mouth somewhere, usually in the front upper part of your mouth—the hard palate. If you just switch the tone to resonate in the back of your mouth on the soft palate, you will be able to change the tone enough for the command to take effect, but not so much that you sound strange.

Here are examples of some embedded commands. The commands are in italics:

- I don't know about *you*, but I *feel excited.*

- I kept calling my dog to *come home with me*, but he wouldn't listen.

- I don't know about *you, Jane*, but I *feel very attracted to* the idea. Is it just *me?*

- A lot of people *become really interested in* magick. For *me* it was *instantly attractive.*

- My clients usually *take my advice*, but you are free to do whatever you want.

Because the deep mind does not recognize negatives easily, you can even embed commands in sentences that indicate the opposite.

- It's probably not good for us to *hook up tonight;* we just met.

- Don't *decide now, Tom*. Take as long as you want.

- Don't *take my word for it;* find out for yourself.

Often these embedded commands work best if your subject is slightly distracted or thrown off his guard by something else. To accomplish this, practitioners will sometimes do something like offer a hand for a handshake then move it away before the target can shake it; this is called a *pattern interrupt.* Another classic is asking someone if a shoe is untied, then quickly hitting them with the embedded command statement. But even if your target isn't off kilter, embedded commands often work wonders.

It has been said that a person's own name is the word that falls sweetest on their ears, so a good way to assist embedded commands is to use the person's name in the command. It's not always possible, but it increases the effect quite a bit. The old occult axiom that to know a true name is to control that being works on many levels.

Of course, we can even further amplify these effects with some of our subtle keys. When you speak, you release breath, and as I mentioned in the first part of the book, breath is the best regulator of magick. In the same way that we accumulated energies and impregnated anchor gestures with them, we can impregnate the breath in as well. To borrow again from Tibetan mantric techniques, you can actually visualize the embedded words forming inside your body then riding out on the breath and entering the person you are targeting. For instance, if trying to win an intellectual argument, you would see the words *agree with me* in your head, then let them release when you say something like: "It's not important that you *agree with me*, it's just good to have the dialogue." If you are trying to make an emotional connection, generate the word at the heart. If you are trying to get laid, generate it a bit lower. . . .

If you are thinking to yourself about how you could possibly be dusting the target with a powder while using these anchors and embedded commands, then you are starting to understand that the blend of mundane and magickal methods makes a great Sorcerer.

Apart from anchors and embedded commands there are lots of other conversational tricks such as *double blinds, tagging questions,* and *yes ladders.* When selling something, rather than asking if your target wants it, ask, *"Do you want that in blue or white?"* This is a double blind. You take the decision out of their hands by replacing it with another decision. Tagging questions are sayings like *"Do you know what I mean?"* or *"Easy, isn't it?"* No one wants to answer these questions in the negative, so they help get someone to agree with you in conversation. Yes ladders are simply batteries of questions that you know a person will answer yes to so that when you get to the main question, they are less likely to change direction and say no. This technique is often used by cold callers and telemarketers, but can be used by anyone. *"Do you consider yourself an adventurous person? Are you spontaneous? Would you like to try out this new program that I am working on?"*

These last three are techniques that I learned when I was a salesman years ago. After I quit making my living that way, I started to realize that we are all salesmen. Everyone needs to get other people to agree to things, no matter who they are. When I started thinking of these techniques in terms of magick, I started to get scary good at it.

I don't have the space here to go through all the techniques one can use to steer a conversation, but I hope that you get the idea of what I am getting at. Using these methods while embedding the target with energies conducive to your goal, and perhaps dusting them with an appropriate condition powder, you can really get a foothold in someone's mind. When this is backed up by the internal work you have been doing on your own identity, and some temple magick by night, you have a full-blown strategy for persuading almost anyone. But before we close the chapter, let's take a look at the influence of deities and spirits.

GETTING THE SPIRIT

Needless to say, there are gods, saints, spirits, and demons that can assist in influencing the minds of others. Some beings aligned with specific types of magick, such as spirits of Venus to help influence lovers, will be covered in later chapters. There are a few forces, however, that are dedicated to pure influence and persuasion, and because I am deeply involved in both the Buddhist and Christian faiths, I thought I might offer examples from those Eastern and Western traditions.

Kurukulla

Kurukulla is a goddess or Dakini that exists not only in Buddhism, but Hinduism as well. She takes several different forms depending upon the text that you are reading, but is always red-skinned, which is the color of Vashya-karma,[3] the magick of bringing people under one's power, often called enchanting or magnetizing action in Buddhist circles. Her four-armed form is the most common one. A description from a Sadhana in my possession reads:

> She is calm and serene, yet passionate and flirtatious,
> possessing the vibrant youth of sixteen summers. In her
> first two hands she draws the bow and arrow of desire, that
> are bedecked and entwined with red hibiscus flowers. In
> her second two hands she folds a noose of lotus root and

Real Sorcery

the iron hook of attraction marked by an unfolding lotus blossom. She is nude and beautifully adorned with jewels and ornaments of human bone. . . .

—*The Short Sadhana for Kurukulla*, translated by John Myrdhin Reynolds

Of course the image of Kurukulla is meant to be sexually exciting to the Tantrika that is working with her, but her symbolism for subduing beings extends beyond that. With her bow and arrow, she strikes her target with specific desires just like Cupid. With her iron hook, she pulls them into her sphere of influence, and with her lotus noose she binds them under her will. There are entire magickal grimoires dedicated to Kurukulla, and they contain spells for everything from curing impotence and constraining husbands to keeping away gray hair and increasing business. She is a useful power to know.

Although there are certain empowerments necessary to practice with Kurukulla as a Tantrika would, there is no reason not to light a red candle, visualize the goddess dancing on a lotus flower in the sky in front of you, and repeat her mantra. The short mantra is the same in the Buddhist and Hindu traditions:

OM KURUKULLA HRI SVAHA!

After repeating the mantra 100, 1,000, or even 10,000 times, ask for her blessing on your spells. I myself have used Kurukulla for everything from charging powders to getting out of speeding tickets.

Saint Martha the Dominator

Martha, the sister of Mary and Lazarus, is mentioned in the Bible in several places, but is most famous for when she cooked for Jesus in her home in Bethany and complained that her sister Mary was not doing any of the work.

But Martha was busy about much serving, who stood and said: Lord, hast Thou no care that my sister hath left me alone to serve? Speak to her therefore, that she help me. And the Lord answering, said to her: Martha, Martha, thou art careful, and art troubled about many things: But one thing is necessary. Mary hath chosen the best part, which shall not be taken away from her.

(Luke: 10:40-42 NRSV)

Though it's not mentioned in scripture, Christian tradition holds that Mary, Lazarus, and Martha made their way to southern France to spread the faith. It was in France, in a town called Nerluc, that Martha supposedly defeated a monster called the Tarasque by feeding him holy water, tying him up in ribbons, and charming him with hymns and prayers. She led the now-tame beast back to town, where it was killed by a blow to the head. The town was renamed Tarascon, and a festival is held there every year to commemorate her deed.

Because of her service to Christ, she is acknowledged as a patron of cooks and servants, and because of her subjugation of the dragon, she is thought of in various occult Christian traditions as a patron of those that need help influencing or dominating others, especially cruel bosses.

To work with her, I recommend getting one of her jar candles, which come in two types. The one that is most commonly available shows Martha dressed in robes and carrying a cross staff, with the dragon subjugated behind her. The other, slightly more exciting form shows an African woman with naturally curly hair, holding a serpent in her hands above her head. Though the latter candle obviously hints at some deeper mysteries of African magick, they are used in the same way. Dress the candle with appropriate oil and pray the following:

Holy Dominatrix Saint Martha,
Who entered the mountain and tied
Up the beast with your ribbons,
I beg you to tie up and dominate [insert name of target].

As you subdued the Tarasque
So that the people of Nerluc could live in peace and
    prosperity
Please subdue [insert name of target]
So that I may have peace and love and prosperity.
Mother, grant me that [insert name of target]
May stand at my feet and obey my will
For the love of God
Grant my petition and eliminate my misery. Amen.

Repeat this for nine nights and let the candle burn all the way down. After Saint Martha comes through for you, you can make Martha an offering. Because she was an evangelist, I have found that the best offering to make to her is to tell others about the work she did for you. You don't have to get specific, but tell enough of the story to magnify her name. You can also donate to a food bank since she served Christ by providing food.

Sometimes people want to do spells involving the saints, but confess to me that they aren't Christian and want to know if it's okay. It's funny how this happens only with Christian figures. Nobody seems to care that they aren't a Buddhist or Hindu to work with Kurukulla or not an ancient Greek to work with Hekate, but because we live in a Christian culture, working magick with the saints or angels can seem more taboo. My advice is this: just do the spell with devotion to deity as you understand it, but do it according to the rules of the tradition from which it comes. In other words, do not call upon Saint Martha in the name of Artemis or Odin. She won't like it. Just as it's impolite to visit a foreign country and demand that everyone follow your customs (though I have seen that often enough), it's impolite to call forth saints and Dakinis and spirits and Loa and whatever into formats with which they aren't comfortable. After you make contact, you can work out some different conditions with the spirit, but don't approach them that way from the start.

REVISITING THE MORAL QUESTION

Now, apart from providing two examples of divine beings used for influencing others, I chose to draw from the Christian and Buddhist traditions for another reason. Both Christianity and Buddhism pride themselves on having exceptionally moral traditions with a focus on peace and compassion. Yet, even in these very ethical traditions, the magick of influence is not considered immoral in and of itself. It can certainly be put to immoral purposes, but so can anything. I hope that I have sufficiently dispelled the strange idea that exists in some quarters of the Pagan and occult community that influencing the mind of another in any way is somehow black magick.

On the other hand, just because it's not *evil* to influence the minds of people around you doesn't make it a good idea. There are people who get really carried away with these techniques, so I want to offer a warning: *do not try to influence everyone in your life.*

There are a lot of people who take NLP classes and are soon bragging about how much of their relations with other people consist of NLP methods. These folks are walking and talking influencing machines that are always on. The same is true of Sorcerers that get so good at influencing others that they want to have everyone under a spell, all the time. They very often are successful at what they attempt, but in the process they lose an important skill: listening and learning.

A large part of love and life is listening, but there are some so bent on convincing others of their points of view that they never take the time to hear anyone else's. It's a shame really, because in the end whatever success they gain is eventually lost when the people around them grow weary of never being heard. So remember Inominandum's rule of influence:

Influencing everyone around you doesn't make you evil.
It makes you a jerk.

IMPLEMENTING THE STRATEGY

Please do not treat this chapter or the chapters that follow it as just another spell book. It's not a reference guide for you to grab one spell from and let it fly. You can do that if you need to; there are certainly enough spells in here, but that's not the intent of the book. The intent is to get you thinking strategically and systematically. Let's take a look at the strategy in sequential steps.

Always start with the inner Sorcery that yields indirect influence. Pick the type of persona you wish to project, study role models, and try their body language and speech patterns on for size. Adopt what you find useful and drop what you don't. Use the Prayer of the Perfected Self in the mornings to reinforce these qualities, and use invocations like the Conjuration of the Commander at night to channel particular energies.

If there are specific people that you need to influence, observe them and make a file. Gather magickal links and think about their dispositions. Find their likes and dislikes so that you can play on them. Influence is a give and take, not just outright domination; play into their dispositions and they will play into your spells.

By day, lay down traps and triggers with powders or talismans that the target will walk over and come into contact with, so that they are surrounded by your influence on a consistent basis.

By night, choose a spell to work from home and get it going late at night when the target is most likely asleep. This could be one of the candle spells, or one of the petition-style spells to a deity, or both.

Learn the arts of magickal conversation. Drop your anchors and issue your embedded commands. Talk visually, kinesthetically, or auditorily to targets based upon their dispositions. Be charming and complimentary but be frank.

Lastly, unless you are deliberately trying to be menacing, for gods' sake, *smile.*

NEW EDITION COMMENTARY—
THOUGHTS ON INFLUENCE

I want to talk just a little more about how your influence should match your situation. Indirect influence, or empowering yourself to be more influential, is almost always the best way to go. There is a marked difference between someone who is trying to gain confidence by convincing and coercion, and someone who simply exudes confidence and influence because they are competent and genuine in who they appear to be.

Direct influence, or magick meant to bend the mind of another person into doing something they probably wouldn't otherwise do, is effective but leaves the target feeling like they've been hornswoggled. Have you ever been convinced to buy something, then you get home wondering why you let yourself get convinced? That's what it feels like. The target of direct influence might not be able to say how they have been coerced or tricked, but they often feel it.

If you are influencing a judge in a court case, or a rival company at a business meeting, you probably don't care about how the target feels. In aggressive and confrontational situations, you just need to win, so go for it.

If, however, you are hoping to build a relationship with someone, be it a lover, an employer, or anyone else that you desire long-term trust with, this is not the way to go about it.

Of course there are many situations that fall between these extremes. Sometimes a Sorcerer will use just enough direct influence to get their foot in the door, and then prove themselves trustworthy, competent, and caring after the fact. In the end, you are the one who has to make these decisions. Just keep in mind that magickal influence has an aftertaste for a target. If it's a brief encounter, it may not matter, but if this this is someone you need to deal with on a regular basis, you need to eventually be able to be the person that you are convincing them that you are.

Real Sorcery

CHAPTER 7

Financial Magick

As I settle down to write this chapter, the world is entering into the largest financial crisis since the great depression. Banks are going belly-up almost daily, the markets are plunging, and people are checking their retirement accounts to find that half the money they had saved and invested is now gone. In short, things are bad. There has never been a time when it was more important to deal with the topic of financial magick.

I chose the term *financial magick* for this chapter, rather than money magick, for a reason: I believe the distinction is very important. There are a lot of money-drawing spells out there; unfortunately they are mostly performed by desperate people in emergencies, or by people hoping for a miracle like winning the lottery. Being able to conjure sums of cash in a hurry is an admirable feat, but the need to do so on a regular basis is the mark of an amateur. Winning the lottery is also okay, but there is so much magick aimed at something so improbable by so many different people, that it's almost impossible for the magick to work. Successful Sorcerers will not be overly concerned with money-drawing magick, but with financial magick, which involves the attraction, management, and distribution of money according to a plan that is sprung from wisdom and cunning.

In fact, using money-drawing magick to react to emergencies can even be dangerous. It is all too easy for even a mediocre Sorcerer to enchant their way into keeping the same crappy job and rundown apartment that they have been stuck in for years. Knowing when it's time to let things fall apart so that you can rebuild from scratch is an important skill. The Alchemical process *solve et coagula*, which means destruction and creation, is important for Sorcerers to internalize. Sometimes the wisest course of action is to do nothing.

Hopefully you won't find yourself in a position where you have to let it all fall apart and restart. This chapter is designed to help you get past that kind of problem. But before we can move to where we want to be financially, we need to examine where we already are.

PERSPECTIVE

I need you to ask yourself a serious question: *Are you wealthy already?*

It's not a trick question. I am not talking about some esoteric definition of wealth like being "rich in friends" or "spiritually wealthy"; I mean it financially. Are you wealthy? I want you to put this book down for a minute and contemplate the question.

I ask this question because perspective in magick is important, but in an age where we can so easily find little pockets of people that are just like us within which to isolate ourselves, it's an especially easy thing to lose. If we spend a good amount of time following the exploits and trials of the rich and famous reported in tabloids, then it's even easier to lose perspective of our own well-being. If we are constantly confronted with images from movies and advertisements that suggest lifestyles of European vacations every year and six-figure wardrobes are the norm, it's really easy to feel poor. Let me throw some numbers out at you:

At the time this was originally written in 2009, anyone making more than $47,500 a year was in the top one percent of income earners on planet earth. If you made more than $25,500 a year, you were in the top ten percent of income earners. The bottom eighty-five percent earned less than $2,185 a year. *Think about that. The bottom fifty percent, half the people on planet earth, lived on less than $800 a year.*

Now, before you start thinking that $25,000 may have been the top in the world, but was still pretty poor for America where the federal poverty line was listed as $10,787 for an individual, let me remind you that we live in a one-world economy. The bottom fifty percent still has no access to services that even the poorest people in industrialized nations do. The bottom twenty-five percent doesn't even have access to potable water on a regular basis. The guy flipping burgers at the local diner may live close to the poverty line in America, but that still makes him amongst the top ten percent wealthiest people on the planet, and his life reflects it.

What does any of this have to do with magick? Am I saying that you should just be happy with what you have and not strive for greater wealth? No, most definitely not. I am all for you attaining greater and greater levels of wealth. If your true will is to heat your thirty-room house by burning twenty-dollar bills while taking a champagne bath in a platinum Jacuzzi then by all means go for it! My point is simply this: you can't just do magick with the aim of being wealthy. If you summon Tzadkiel, the archangel of Jupiter, and ask him to make you wealthy, he is just going to look at you funny and remind you that you are probably already in the top ten percent, if not the top one percent. If, however, you ask him to help you and present him with a detailed plan that will result in greater wealth, he is probably going to be a lot more helpful. You need perspective about where you are, where you want to be, and a plan to get from one to the other.

MONEY AS SPIRIT

In the Bible, Christ refers to money as an entity named Mammon. The word *Mammon* is still in use today as a word for "money" in Finnish, Hebrew, Dutch, Czech, German, and a whole host of other languages. The characterization of money as a spiritual entity is a good one, and an important one for Sorcerers to understand. Money has all the characteristics of a spirit, as surely as a demon in a medieval grimoire. Money, like a spirit, is intangible and invisible: cash and computerized accounts only represent money as talismans and rituals—they are not money itself. Despite its intangible nature, it can create very concrete effects in people's lives by its presence or absence. Money requires certain offerings and has certain protocols for handling it if you want it to remain friendly. If money is mistreated, it will leave as surely as an offended guest. If you become too invested in it, it can possess you as if you were Linda Blair.[1]

Whether money acts as an angelic or demonic spirit is largely in how you handle it. This is where Christ's advice about Mammon comes in: "You cannot serve both God and Mammon." This doesn't mean that Mammon is in and of itself evil, just that you cannot serve Mammon. It must serve you. This is no different from the ceremonial magician's evocation of demons. When evoking a demon, you bind them to oaths and make them submit to your will, which is aligned to the divine will. They must serve you, not the other way around. You are, in fact, fulfilling the natural order of the universe by commanding the demons in the name of divine will, and thus exposing them to the divine light. Money is no different—tame it and make it serve you or you will end up its servant, or worse, its victim.

As an example, I know a hedge fund manager that is quite rich. However, I would not call him wealthy because he is a slave to his money. Working eighty or ninety hours a week will make you a lot of money in the right profession, but working so much that you have no time to enjoy it outside of drinking yourself into oblivion every weekend is not wealth.

On the other end of the spectrum are people who are not able to handle money at all. They don't know how to get it, and even when they get some, they can't hang on to it. According to wealth counselor Szifra Birke, about one third of lottery winners find themselves in serious financial trouble or in bankruptcy within just five years of winning.[2] Many end up worse off than they were before winning. Wealth used unwisely can wreak havoc. The larger the amount, the more damage it can do.

It's important that you develop a healthy and balanced relationship with money. Many people involved in modern neo-Pagan movements, magick, and other spiritual paths tend to be so anti-materialist that they develop unhealthy relationships with money itself. A friend of mine who is both an occultist and a successful businessman was once asked on a forum how he can resolve being a spiritual person while still holding a high-paying job for a major corporation. Although some spiritual paths do focus on poverty as a path, most do not. It's a bit cliché but you really can be "in the world but not of it." If you fear or mistrust money, then I would recommend working on that. It will cause you just as many problems as if you were obsessively materialistic. Bring it on the path. Learn to like money, and treat it with respect. It will do the same to you.

BASIC FINANCIAL WISDOM

I hope that by now you are realizing that I am not going to be offering any instant spells to win the lottery or get set for life. That is the kind of magick marketed to the gullible and desperate, not for the serious modern Sorcerer. Because understanding the nature of money and the methods of building wealth is so important to financial magick, it is imperative that before we get into the spells and rituals that we spend a bit more time on basic financial knowledge.

There are hundreds of books out there on personal financial planning, but for the most part they all focus on a few basic points that can be boiled down to a few simple rules. Most of them will seem obvious, yet increasingly few people put them into action. None of them are particularly deep. We won't be covering advanced economics here, just some simple axioms that will help you focus your mundane and magickal efforts at building wealth.

First Rule: Spend Less than You Earn.
Everyone has a pile of money coming in and a pile of money going out. If the pile coming in is bigger than the pile going out, you will build wealth. If the pile of money going out is bigger than the pile of money coming in, you will build debt. It's that simple. The amount of money in the piles has almost nothing to do with the process. There are people who make six or seven figures and can't make ends meet, and people near the poverty line who manage to save a little bit for retirement. For examples of rich people who fail because of not recognizing this simple rule just turn on one of the many "where are they now" type shows in VH1 or E!.

Second Rule: Earn More.
Because the first rule is to spend less than you earn it only makes sense that the next step in increasing wealth is obviously to increase what you earn. This can be accomplished in many ways. You can get promoted at the job you have. Investing in education can often help in this and is one of the few acceptable debts that will help you build wealth in the long run.

Another possibility is to seek out a new job or career that will offer more advancement. Education can also be important on this route as well, but so is networking with people. Social networking is key in building wealth, and you should always strive to keep good relations with people from former jobs and maintain at least some connection with old friends. Organized groups can also be helpful;

I know someone who joined the Freemasons specifically for the possibility of advancing his career. He considers his dues to be money well spent.

Even if you have a successful career, it never hurts to have a secondary income stream. In uncertain times like these, it seems like entire industries can go sour in an instant. Having a side business will help you stay afloat in bad times and provide an added bonus in good times. Some people get to do the thing that they love as their main career, but most of us don't. Society just isn't set up for everyone to have a job that they love. A second job is a great way to turn a hobby or an interest that would ordinarily cost you money into something that makes you money. At the end of the book, I will talk about going pro as a Sorcerer and making money off magick directly.

Third Rule: Spend Less.
Just as you increased the pile of money coming in by earning more you need to always work to decrease the pile of money going out. Again, it seems obvious, but a large part of the current economic crisis is due to people living beyond their means. Examine habits that cost you money and break some of them. I am not saying that you shouldn't enjoy yourself or spend money, but keep it to what you can afford. There was a time when credit card companies wouldn't give you limits that you could never pay back and banks would not let you take out mortgages that are beyond your means. Now, it's the reverse. They will take the shovel with which you dig your hole of debt with and replace it with a backhoe. You need to know what you can afford and stick to it. Just because your credit rating is good does not mean that you can afford a million-dollar house, no matter what the banker tells you. It's a radical idea, I know, but it really is okay to just buy what you can pay for.

If you are currently having difficulties or are trying to jump start your savings, I would be willing to bet that you can do with less. You don't need Starbucks, HBO, or all those magazines. Evan Lansing, a blogger from Michigan, spent a month eating on a dollar a day in 2006. He lost weight, was healthier, and ended up a little bit wealthier than when he started. If he can do that, surely you can make a few cuts here and there. You will be amazed at the things that you won't miss once you give them up.

Fourth Rule: Manage Your Money Wisely.
If you follow the first three rules, you will start to accumulate money. The fourth rule focuses on changing the ways that you manage that money. If you have high interest debt, consolidate it. Look for a low-interest card to put it on, then focus on paying it off. Get rid of credit cards that you don't need, and use the ones that you keep as sparingly as possible. I use mine only for travel and pay for everything else with cash.

After you kill your debt, it's time to max out retirement benefits. If your company contributes to a 401k, be sure that you give enough to get the full match. It's a guaranteed win for you. Other investments are up to you. Different advisers like different approaches. The only advice I will give is to make sure that you diversify. In the early 2000s, many friends of mine lost everything they had when the tech bubble burst. Recently, some more friends are losing their savings in the sub-prime mess. Keep your investments diverse and you won't go too wrong.

The Last Rule: Think about What You Really Want.
Financial magick and wealth building in general are not about getting rich by someone else's standards, they're about freedom to do things that you like. I will tell you now that if your primary goal in life is to be filthy rich, magick is not the way to accomplish it. If money were all I loved, I would have become a banker or broker. I would be working eighty-hour weeks, but I would be rich. That's not how I choose to live my life, though, and not how most Sorcerers and magicians live. Money for most people is a means to an end, not the end itself.

I currently have a day job that pays an amount that I am happy with, as well as a few other income streams that help me out. *Thanks for purchasing this book, by the way.* I am not as wealthy as some, but it's enough. My day job is low stress and allows significant opportunity for me to continue my practice throughout the day. That, to me, is wealth.

I have one friend who used magick to secure a very high-paying job in New York that he is quite happy with. He is wealthy by almost any standard. Another friend of mine lives near the poverty line, but is happy because he works doing only what he loves: reading cards on Jackson Square in New Orleans. He may not be wealthy by most people's standards, but he is by mine. Decide what is right for you, then accomplish it.

THE PLANETS

Now that we have covered some basic financial knowledge, it's time to look at the magickal forces that we will be harnessing in our work. Let's start with the planets. Most people correctly associate Jupiter with wealth magick, but that is only half the equation. In financial magick, you need the power of both Jupiter and Mercury at your disposal. Jupiter is the mass of wealth, but Mercury is the movement. Think of it like this: *Jupiter is your savings account; Mercury is your checking account.* You need them both.

Here then is a preliminary blessing that involves both powers. It can be used as a stand-alone prayer or incorporated into other rituals.

INVOCATION OF MERCURY AND JUPITER SPIRITS

IAO, AOI, OIA, AIO, IOA, OAI
By the permutation of the highest name

I call forth the spheres of Jupiter and Mercury
May the Jovian sphere of Grace and Glory
And the Mercurial splendor of Lamprotesis[3]
Work hand in hand to promulgate prosperity
By IOPHIEL and TIRIEL
By the letters E and OO
I stir, summon, and bind the spirits of the spheres
HISMAEL arise!
Garner, glory, and gain the blessing of wealth and power
TAPHTHARTHARATH!
Motivate and move the powers of prosperity about me and
 through me,
As Mercury issued forth from the seed of Jove
May movement and accretion work in union.
That affluence and riches may flow forth
And return increased a thousandfold
In the name of the Highest
IAO, AOI, OIA, AIO, IOA, OAI

THE CASHBOX

A great way to work with the interplay of Jupiter and Mercury is
the cashbox. Get yourself a cheap wood box that is big enough to
hold a good amount of papers and items. It doesn't need to be huge;
mine is 6 × 3 × 3 inches. Carve, engrave, or paint the symbols of
the planet, intelligence, and spirit of Jupiter on the front of the box.
Put four Jupiterian astrological symbols on the lid along with one
of the pentacles of Jupiter from the key of Solomon—the choice is
yours. On the inside of the lid, place the Kamea of Jupiter. Paint or
stain the box an appropriate color, such as blue for Jupiter or gold
for wealth. Rub the outside of the whole box with money-drawing
oil and the inside of the box with money-keeping oil. Pay special

attention to rubbing the oil into the symbols you carved or painted onto the box.

After you have constructed the box, go to the place where you do your banking and take a little dirt from the land just outside the bank. If you live in a city and there is no natural ground outside the bank, then you can take some dust from the bank or even some dirt from a potted plant. Line the bottom of the cashbox with the dirt. You can place other symbolic items in the box as well. I have in mine:

- A gator's hand for "grabbing" money and opportunity.

- Sassafras leaves for holding onto money I get.

- A lodestone for attracting money.

- Irish moss, allspice, cinnamon, and other money-drawing herbs.

Next, take some cash and dress each bill up with Mercurial symbols: four on each side, making eight in total—the number of Mercury. On a Thursday morning, perform the invocation of Jupiter/ Mercury over the box and cash. Place the cash in the box and leave it in the box for a week. You can add more cash as you see fit. Next Thursday, take the cash out of the box and spend it. The idea here is that the cash is now a talisman and will attract more cash to you, which you then place into the box. It you do it right, you should be able to soon afford to place more cash into the box, thus increasing the amount that returns, just like any good investment.

THE LONG-TERM PETITION

The cashbox is a wonderful tool to keep empowering the money that flows through your life, and to build upon it, but it's also necessary to get that wealth to flow according to a plan. For this I recommend the long-term petition, a sort of talismanic financial plan.

Go back to the financial wisdom section above and think about the steps I outlined in terms of your own life. Think about where you want to be when you retire, even if you are in your early twenties and it seems like a lifetime away.[4] Think about the job you have and the career you would like to have. Think about ways to make money other than your day job. Think about the freedom that you would like to have for yourself. Then sit down and make a plan for the next year.

I actually like to do this petition on New Year's Day, but any day will do. Write out your plan like a letter to the gods. Be specific about things that you would like to work on during the next year, and opportunities that you would like to open up. Write it all down and then fold it up and place it on a metal plate, preferably tin, the metal of Jupiter. If you want to decorate the petition with sigils and oils, then you should do so.

Next, take a lodestone, the largest you can find, and cleanse it with some whiskey to remove any psychic patterns from it. Place it on the petition and pray the following:

By the great name IAO
I stir, summon, and call thee
O thee powers of earth.
Arise and take up residence within this stone
As I fulfill you with offerings of iron
May you fulfill me with offerings of wealth
Act according to the will and words that support you.
As I fulfill you, so you fulfill me.
So it is written, so it shall be.

Every week, or even every day if you can keep up with it, you should sprinkle some iron grit on the stone. As the grits are attracted to the stone, the powers in the stone will attract the events and wishes expressed in the petition. As you make your offerings, utter a little prayer to keep it going.

At the end of the year, and every year after that, change the petition to accommodate changing circumstances. Bury your old petitions on your property to symbolize that their blessings are now part of your life. If the wishes in the petition change drastically, for instance you decide you do not want something that you asked for in the petition, or you change your career direction, simply perform a small offering of thanks to the powers that you have summoned into the stone. Clean it with whiskey and start again with a new petition.

FINANCIAL ALTARS

Unlike some other issues that you will tackle occasionally with Sorcery, such as finding a lover or dealing with a court case, you will be dealing with financial issues until the day that you die. Even if you manage to strike it filthy rich, you will need to manage your money wisely. Because of this many Sorcerers find it useful to erect permanent wealth altars.

Whether it's a large and ornate altar worthy of a temple, or a discreet corner of a bookshelf, a permanent altar acts as a sort of psychic control panel and energy generator. Symbolic items placed upon the altar will manifest in your life, even those placed there accidentally, so it's imperative that you keep it clean and free of clutter that doesn't relate to the work the altar is devoted to.

To make your own altar, simply decide how much space you can afford to devote to it, then clean it off and place a green, blue, or gold altar cloth on it to demarcate the space as sacred. Place any wealth-related effigies, amulets, talismans, or sorcerous paraphernalia on the altar and arrange them according to your inner guidance. Perform a brief consecration of your own devising. For example, you could use the invocation of Mercury and Jupiter that I provided, then follow it up with a request to bless the altar before you.

Amongst the items on my financial altar are:

- A large print of Dzambhala, the Buddhist deity of wealth.

- A statue of Saint Expedite, a saint who is great at getting things done fast.

- Several green and gold candles burning for various clients.

- The cashbox.

- A box containing banking information on various account investments with the sigil of Tzadkiel, the archangel of Jupiter, upon it.

- A bottle that contains a familiar spirit who works on money matters for me.

- My long-term petition and lodestone.

- A bottle containing some graveyard dirt from a relative who was a great businessman.

SHORT-TERM SPELLS

As much as I am in favor of careful financial magick rather than reactionary money-drawing spells, emergencies do sometimes occur. Using some of the previous techniques, as well as careful implementation of the influencing techniques from the last chapter on key figures in your workplace, will help mitigate the need for emergency magick, but the need does occasionally arise.

THE MONEY-DRAWING LIGHT

Probably the most common and easiest spell that you can do for yourself or others is to set a light on your financial altar. First make a petition stating exactly what you need to happen and place it on your altar. Get an appropriately colored candle: green or gold for money, blue for Jupiter, and so on. Dress the candle with appropriate oil such as money drawing, Money Stay with Me, Jupiter oil, or even just some spearmint oil. Hold the base of the candle toward your body and rub the oil on from the top towards the base, drawing it toward you. If you are using a glass-encased candle then use a drill bit to make seven holes in the wax and fill them with the oil. Place the candle on the petition and invoke over the candle to whatever powers you hold dear.

Let the candle burn and observe how it burns. If it keeps going out, then it may indicate a rough time with that issue. If it starts off smoky, then burns clear, it may indicate some unwanted consequences at first, but eventual success. Watch for patterns and images in the wax and use your divination skills to interpret them, even using sortilege and augury to interpret the omens in the candle.

Traditionally you would leave the candle burning until it goes out, however I cannot in good conscience recommend doing this. It would be nice to think that the spirits would protect the candle from setting the house on fire, but my friends at the fire department tell me otherwise. If you have to extinguish the candle, I recommend the following prayer as you do so:

> May this light burn brightly on the higher planes
> And continue to dispel the darkness it has been set against
> Until I can relight it again safely here in the physical.
> So shall it be.

A MONEY-DRAWING HAND

There are literally hundreds of recipes for mojo hands and gris-gris bags to draw money. One of my favorites is to place sixteen allspice berries along with some cinnamon, Irish moss, chamomile, cinquefoil, sunflower seeds, and a piece of High John into a green bag or cloth. Pray the Twenty-Third Psalm or a similar prayer of abundance and then place three of your own hairs in the bag. Feed the bag with an appropriate oil or with whiskey.

FOR AN EXACT SUM

If mojo hands and herbs are not your thing, then you can appeal directly to the spirits of earthly treasure by writing them a letter. Write out the exact sum of money that you need and take it to a crossroads. Pore breathe the element earth so that you resonate with the element that you want to work with. Make an offering as per the usual means. Be sure to bring a libation of whiskey with you, and pour it directly on the ground. Feed elemental earth into the liquid as you do so. Ask the gnomes, Shidak, and other spirits of the ground to help you by bringing to you the sum of money you need. Bury the paper that you wrote the sum of money on, and then walk away without looking back. This works exactly the same way as the lead defixiones tablets from ancient Greece, only here we are appealing to the benevolent side of the chthonic powers and asking for a boon rather than a curse.

Summoning Demons

Sometimes angels and planetary intelligences are a bit too lofty for our needs. We may need that kind of spiritual strength behind us, but just a little more earthbound in execution. In times like these, there is nothing like the aid of a demon.

Now, don't freak out on me here. I am not suggesting we make pacts with Lucifer or deal with truly evil spirits. I am saving that stuff for another book. The word *demon* is simply a corruption of the Greek word *daemon*, which means spirit. In this case, the distinction between angels and demons is not one of good versus evil, but of being heavenly versus earthly, or to use the technical occult term: sublunar.

Sublunar spirits are useful because they tend to deliver what is asked for quickly and with little fuss. The danger is that while an angel might decide to not grant a request if it is something that might impede your growth or spiritual path, the sublunar spirit will get you what you ask for exactly. They also tend to act faster than angelic beings, though angelic results often stretch further into the future. It's up to you to know what you need and to want what you ask for. I have worked with demons quite a lot and have never had any kind of negative backlash or evil spring up because of it. I have occasionally had to deal with not really thinking through what I asked for, but that's not the spirit's fault. Read again through the financial wisdom section and keep your requests in line with your overall plan.

That said, you do need to be able to summon and constrain the demon. Ideally you would have the Knowledge and Conversation of your Agathodaimon when summoning a demon; however, if you are adept at the Universal Center exercise, are regular in your invocations, and competent at banishing, you should have no trouble.

The demon that I am going to recommend is quite friendly and well-disposed toward working with Sorcerers. Bune is the twenty-sixth spirit in that most famous grimoire: the Goetia. Of course the spirits in the Goetia are not unique to only that book. Most of them appear in a very early scripture called *The Testament of Solomon* and in other grimoires such as the *Pseudomonarchia Daemonum*. Bune is a spirit that has dominion over burial and the dead, but is also excellent at bestowing riches and honors. I have worked with Bune in the past, as have several friends of mine. Frater R. O., the proprietor of the *Head for the Red* blog, has an ongoing permanent project involving Bune and a spirit pot that he made for him.

To summon Bune in times of need, you should first draw his seal on a piece of paper that you will then suspend from a string around your neck. The string should be long enough that you can pick up the seal and hold it in front of your eyes without removing it from around your neck. Banish the area and consecrate a circle on the ground by tracing a circle about you with a wand or your fingertip. As you do so, speak the following prayer:

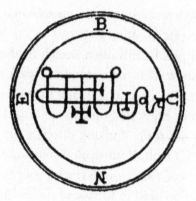

The Seal of Bune

Gyrum Carpo! (I take/seize the circle!)
Consecro et Benedico istum circulum (I consecrate and
    bless this circle)
per nomina dei attisimi IAO (in the name of the most
    powerful god IAO)

Burn some incense as an offering and look at the seal of Bune. Conjure him with the following words:

IAO, AOI, OIA, AIO, IOA, OAI
"I have called unto thee with all my heart,
Hear me, O lord, and I shall seek my justification."
Bune! Bune! Bune!
I call to thee in the name of the most high god IAO
Come forth from thy abode and appear at the edge of my
    circle.

By the angel Haajah, I call and conjure thee.
By the power of Vehrin and Sagan, I stir and summon thee.
Come forth and offer me aid in my time of need
Set thy thirty legions of Bunis to work for me
And I shall glorify thy name and make your
   deeds known.

That's all you really need. The powers that constrain him are included in the conjuration. I explain the name IAO in Appendix 1. The lines that follow are from Psalm 118, which Dr. Thomas Rudd, a prominent Scholar Magician of the 17th century, has associated with Bune. Haajah is the angel of the Shemhamphorash that corresponds to Bune. Vehrin and Sagan are the Greek and Egyptian names of the second decan of Sagittarius, who rules over Bune. If you like, you can use one of the gazes in the first part of the book to try and *see* Bune at the edge of your circle, but this is not necessary. You will probably feel his presence come at once, but if not, then simply repeat the part of the conjuration that starts with *Bune! Bune! Bune!* Keep calling until you feel his presence.

Once you have a sense that you have gotten Bune's attention, simply make your requests. Be fair but firm. Do not ask for millions of dollars. Ask for reasonable requests and he will probably grant them. In the last part of the conjuration, you promise to glorify his name. This is a type of offering whereby you make the spirit more famous and powerful. If you like working with Bune, you should consider engraving his seal on copper, which in itself can be a type of offering to the spirit. You can tell others about the work he has done for you as an offering for services rendered, which is exactly what I have done by including this section in the book, fulfilling my own promise to the spirit.

When your congress with Bune is complete, you should politely signal the end of the session with the following dismissal:

I thank you for your attendance at this rite. As you came in power, go forth in peace, ever ready to come again should I call. In the name of IAO, the temple is duly closed.

The Goetia recommends a rather involved and prop-heavy ceremony for summoning the demons, and it is my hope that my readers will not interpret the very brief and simple summoning to mean that I consider the grimoire's instructions to be useless. Far from it. The truth is that any spirit can be communicated with using nothing more than its name and seal, but the full ceremony will result in a much stronger and profound connection. It's like the difference between watching TV using an old antenna from the 1960s versus fiber-optic HD. I would encourage any readers who have a good experience working with Bune to study the Goetia in depth, and attempt the experiments as they were written. This is, however, a bit is beyond the scope of the present chapter.

THE STRATEGY

I hope that you have realized that the information in the previous two chapters can be just as vital to financial magick as anything else in this chapter. Use your intelligence-gathering skills to review investments, look for rough spots in the economy, and to foresee unfortunate circumstances that will impact your job or nest egg. You should also use the influencing magick from the last chapter to help you in job interviews or advance your interests at work. Everything in this book, and in magick in general, relates to everything else. Chapters and divisions exist only for ease of understanding.

Remember, this book isn't a spell book; it's a field guide. I want to outline a basic strategy and give a few examples of how to implement that strategy. It's up to you either to use the spells and rituals as given, to change them according to your needs, or to seek out others that will fulfill the requirements of the strategy.

Now let's tie all of this into a tight strategy for success:

The first step is to assess where you are. Write it all down, listing every asset and liability you possess. Leave nothing out. Next look at the two piles of money: the one coming in and the one going out. Think about how you can increase the first pile and decrease the second. Use the invocation of Jupiter and Mercury as a prayer to aid you in your thinking and inspire ideas. Your plan should answer the following questions:

- Am I in the profession I really want to be in?

- If so, how do I advance myself further and faster?

- If not, how do I get the education and retraining I need for a different path?

- How many hours do I really want to devote to my job per week?

- How can I cut back on my spending? What do I really enjoy versus just do out of habit?

- What secondary income streams can I cultivate?

- How can I schedule payments to eliminate all my debts in reasonable amounts of time?

- Which debts should be paid off first?

- When will I retire, and how much money will I need in order to continue living in the style that I am used to?

If this seems like a lot of work, that's because it is. But it is necessary work in order to be a genuine master of financial magick and not just someone who summons cash as a reaction to emergencies. If you don't deal with these questions, they will be dealt with for you. That is not the way that a Sorcerer behaves.

Next, set up your financial altar. Make your cashbox and set your lodestone and petition to work. Make regular offerings to the local spirits, especially the spirits of the earth. Keep the altar clean and honor the powers that are represented upon it. If your Sorcery honors the gods, the gods will honor your Sorcery.

Set lights, make mojo hands, and even summon demons to help implement specific parts of your plan. You should go into every interview and meeting with the boss armed with the influencing magick from the last chapter. If you need money for school or to get rid of a particularly perfidious debt, summon Bune and ask for his help. And of course, if after all your careful planning the need for emergency funds still crops up, and it will, by all means do some spells to draw some quick cash. Just don't make it a habit.

NEW EDITION COMMENTARY—
FINANCIAL SORCERY

I am so passionate about financial Sorcery that I wrote a whole book about it. It is also something that a lot of people in the Pagan and occult communities struggle with. I am not just talking about the usual financial struggles that most people have, I am talking about avoiding money and talk of money, and framing it as something that spiritual and magickal people should not be concerned with.

Here is the problem: Money is too important to ignore. You *must* master it, or it will master you.

If you want an anti-materialist spirituality, that's great, but you need to really do it. Become a monk or nun, a wandering yogi, or part of an off-grid community. Non-materialist spirituality is a serious endeavor; working a string of dead-end jobs while complaining about consumerism is not dealing with the issue. You will find yourself spending even more time making ends meet and worrying about money than people who deal with it as a part of life.

If you don't want to get serious about renouncing money and materialism, then you should get serious about your own strategy for dealing with money. This does not mean becoming as rich as you can, or becoming driven by the almighty dollar. On the contrary, it is about making enough money, and managing it well so that you don't have to be constantly concerned about it. No one is more obsessed with money than someone who has to choose between a car repair and rent.

In this chapter, I laid out five rules for financial magick, but I actually don't think they hold up very well. "Spend less" for instance is not very useful advice. You can cut only so much, whereas there is no cap on how much you can earn. Even when you are in dire straits and can't afford basic necessities, the occasional splurge on a treat might make life just a little bit more bearable and give you the energy and motivation to soldier on.

Your financial strategy should change depending upon what stage you are at. I divide financial wellness into four stages: Stuck, Solvent, Solid, and Sovereign.

1. Stuck: Your income does not meet your necessary expenses. While you shouldn't make too many frivolous expenditures at this stage, watching spending should not be your main concern either. You need to make more money. Period. Increasing income should be your focus. Not saving, not investing, not cutting back on lattes: just make more money.

2. Solvent: You have enough money to cover expenses. Just enough. When people talk about living hand-to-mouth, this is what they are talking about. Of course you want to keep increasing your income at this point, but this is also the point at which watching your spending becomes vital. As I mentioned in the chapter, you can live hand-to-mouth at any income level. If you increase your spending to meet your higher income, you will never get ahead of the game.

3. Solid: Your income more than covers your expenses, you have six months to a year of emergency funds, and you are making investments to grow wealth. Your main task here is to make your money make money. You can focus on investing in the market, purchasing moneymaking assets, or owning small businesses that you don't have to work at day to day.

4. Sovereign: You have more money than you and your family reasonably need even with investments. This is where you are building legacy through how you disperse your wealth. Some will focus on philanthropic and charitable ventures. Others will fund research or build companies. Still others will simply become plutocrats, hoarding as much as they can.

I myself am firmly in solid territory, but it was not always so. I spent most of my twenties as "stuck," focusing magick on dealing with emergencies and getting by. When I finally decided to get serious about money, it didn't take long for me to become solvent, then firmly solid.

Knowing where you are at is important because something that makes sense at one level will be poison at another. When you are solid, you can get a credit card that offers amazing rewards, another way for your money to make money. The interest rate doesn't matter much because you pay it off, in full, every month. Someone that is stuck or solvent, though, should focus on getting a low-interest card rather than one that offers high rewards because they might have to carry a balance from one month to the next.

Just remember: it's not only magick that matters, it's what you aim it at.

CHAPTER 8

Protection and Security

The topic of magickal protection and security is so important that I dedicated my entire first book to it. *Protection and Reversal Magick* (New Page Books, 2006; revised edition, Weiser Books, 2023) presents an entire strategy for defensive magick that ranges from simple protection spells, to exorcism rites, to advanced methods of magickal combat. Though I cannot cover the topic in the same depth in the course of this chapter, the present work would be incomplete if I did not include a chapter on protection and security within it. This also gives me the opportunity to clarify the earlier work, as well as present the essence of the strategy in a more condensed format.

The first question that must be answered is, of course, who or what are we defending ourselves against? There are two main categories of danger that Sorcerers might face: physical and occult. The physical dangers are those that anyone might face: accidents, harm from criminals, personal enemies, and so on. Occult dangers can originate from one of four sources: stumbling unprepared into places of power and being negatively affected by their ambiance, missteps or broken vows in our occult practice, offended spirits acting in retribution for offensive actions, and deliberate attacks from other practitioners.

SYMPTOMS OF OCCULT DANGER

Unless you are being stalked by a stranger, in most cases of physical danger the source should be fairly obvious. Occult danger is, by definition, hidden. We can, however, look for certain symptoms. I divide symptoms into three basic categories:

1. External conditions.

2. Mental conditions.

3. Physical conditions.

External Conditions

Attacks of this nature affect the probabilities of events, or luck, in a person's life, creating what is known as "crossed conditions." This often starts with a mild feeling of being out of step with time, as if you can no longer manage to be in the right place at the right time. This can be accompanied by patterns of bad luck, and of everything you touch going wrong. Not just one fender bender in your car, but several in the space of a few days. Left alone, things get worse: you lose your job, your lover leaves you, you wreck the car, you are blamed for something you didn't do, and perhaps even wind up in jail or worse. The possibilities of what can happen are limited only by the power of the person or power launching the attack, and how long you let it go on. Almost everything that happens will have a completely rational and material explanation. Taken alone, they don't mean anything. Taken together, a long string of unfortunate coincidences should be a good indicator that something is amiss.

This is especially true if these external conditions are accompanied by some of the following mental and physical symptoms.

Mental Conditions

Most magickal and psychic attacks manifest mental symptoms in their targets. I previously mentioned the feeling of being "out of step with time" as being a precursor to crossed conditions. There are other more serious mental symptoms that can arise as well. Some attacks such as telepathic or hypnotic attacks may have *only* mental effects. By far the most common mental symptom is a feeling of despair, oppression, anxiety, and fear without any identifiable cause. Inexplicable confusion or moments where you cannot focus are common. Troubled dreams are also a sign of attack.

In cases where coercive magick is being used to influence your actions, either through hypnosis, telepathic control, or a spell, you may experience uncharacteristic compulsions, and affinities or aversions to things that you never did before. It is very difficult to notice this on your own because the mind tends to justify these feelings as natural, but if friends and loved ones are saying that you are acting out of character, then you should at least take a few moments and consider what they have to say.

Left untreated, mental symptoms of magickal attack can, and have, led people deep into psychosis and insanity. There is no telling how many people suffering from mental illness have a magickal or spiritual component to their pain. What is important for the Sorcerer to keep in mind, though, is that if they are experiencing or are protecting someone with these kinds of serious mental problems, a trained psychologist or psychiatrist must be involved in the treatment. In ancient times, the village Shaman or Witch doctor was the mental health professional, but it's not that way any longer. In all cases of danger, contact the appropriate authorities.

Physical Conditions

There can also be physical symptoms associated with attack. Headaches are a common early warning. Headaches where the scalp feels stretched too thin over the skull are particularly indicative of attack. Sometimes when we lie down to sleep, these aches will gather to one side of the head, indicating the direction that the attack is coming from.

After headaches, fatigue would be the next most common occurrence. This is particularly true in cases of parasitic and vampiric attacks. In parasitic cases, someone of weak constitution and energy psychically drains someone that possesses higher vitality. This is most often unintentional and occurs commonly between family members or close friends, particularly when one is in the position of caring for the other, thus giving rise to the old adage that "the caregiver goes first."

When spirits are used in an attack, or when they are themselves on the attack as in a haunting, the most common complaint I have heard is of a weight on the chest when sleeping. This is sometimes called "hag riding" and occurs so commonly that there has recently been a study of the phenomenon by a professor at the University of Pennsylvania (*The Terror That Comes in the Night*, David J. Hufford). Sometimes feelings of sexual violation accompany this sensation.

A sudden but persistent illness can also be the result of an attack. From a sudden but simple flu, to serious cancer, to completely undiagnosable illnesses, curses have the power to affect the physical shell directly. In very potent attacks by powerful forces, medical events such as heart attacks and aneurisms can be the result of psychic attack, but these instances are exceedingly rare.

Loss of sexual interest and impotency can be the result of a jinx by a jealous or jilted lover. Spells for taking away "sexual nature" exist in almost all types of folk magick around the world, as do methods of restoring that nature.

OMENS AND WARNINGS

Apart from the actual symptoms of an attack, there are omens to watch for, first among them being dreams. The Oneiric realm is where our deep mind tries to communicate with the rest of the self. There is no one symbol set to interpret dreams for everyone. The serpent that means fear in your dream might symbolize magickal power in mine. Pay attention to how your dreams make you *feel*, then interpret the events in that light. If you are talented at Oneiric magick, you can sometimes divine the name of the culprit from the dream.

There are ways that a Sorcerer can set up early warning systems to alert him of an attack before it gets very serious. The first and easiest method is to have a plant or two in each room of the house. If you are under magickal attack, it is almost a guarantee that the plants will suffer first. For this reason, many Witches keep live plants all over the house.

Keeping a fresh egg on the altar can not only help indicate an attack, but absorb some of it as well. Like the plants, an egg will take the hit of negative energy for you and go bad quickly or even break in the event of an attack.

This list of symptoms is by no means exhaustive. There is an endless variety of attacks that can be launched and just as many symptoms that can occur. What is important to realize is that, taken individually, everything that happens may have a logical "real world" explanation. Many of these symptoms and events all occurring within a short time, however, is a good indicator of a genuine attack. Remember to err on the side of caution and not ignore the symptoms when they occur.

PERSONAL PROTECTION

If you perform the regular practices in the first part of this book such as meditation, invocation, offerings, and the occasional banishing or framing rite, this will provide almost all the protection you will need as a Sorcerer. There will, however, be times when you need to address a situation directly and with stronger stuff than just your regular practice. You may also find yourself in the position of helping a non-practitioner who has no regular spiritual practice clear away crossed conditions and attacks, in which case you will need to employ amulets and other more protection-specific modes of practice.

Amulets

Amulets are physical objects that protect one from harm or drive away specific forces. They are used in almost every culture on earth and take innumerable forms from the lucky rabbit's foot to extremely complex Kabbalistic scrolls. Unlike a shield, the beauty of an amulet is that you never have to think about it; it's always on. This also makes it ideal for helping people that may feel they are being psychically attacked, but are not Sorcerers themselves and are thus unlikely to project shields, perform banishings, and the like.

In my book *Protection and Reversal Magick*, you will find a short list of traditional protective amulets from all over the world, as well as several different rituals for specific amulets. In this chapter, I want to approach the subject from a looser perspective and teach a more universal method of working with protective amulets. As with everything in this book, you should relate what I am teaching here to other chapters. The methods used for protection amulets can easily be turned toward love charms and wealth talismans.

The skilled Sorcerer has the power to charge just about anything as an amulet. Some things hold a charge better than others, of course. When choosing an object to charge as an amulet, you should look at both the material and the symbolism. Natural materials work better than purely synthetic ones. Plastic, for instance, has many wonderful properties, but is not a good "fluid condenser," to borrow a term from Franz Bardon. Wood, metal, stone, and other natural materials seem to accept a charge just fine. I have met people who have charged electronic devices encased in plastic, but in this case it is the mostly metal insides that hold the charge, not the plastic.

Certain metals, minerals, and woods have magickal properties in and of themselves. Of all materials, iron, the metal of Mars, is the ultimate apotropaic substance and is recognized all over the world for its abilities to interrupt spells, harm Witches, and drive away or even kill harmful spirits. Silk-cotton wood is the most powerful cleansing and protecting wood in Palo, where it is known as Siguaya Palo. Rowan is considered the best exorcism wood in many traditions of European craft.

The symbolism of the object is also important. Crosses, pentagrams, Stars of David, and other religious icons of course make excellent protective charms. Other cultural protective items such as the Hamsa hand, Mano Cornuto, and swastika can also be powerful hosts for protective power. The symbolism need not be traditional, however. I once empowered a child's toy soldier as a protective amulet, and have a friend that went around his house and made every alarm sensor into an amulet. Symbolism is helpful, but not necessary. If you have an item that you love to wear or carry, but it doesn't have any symbolism that you can think of, you can still charge it.

There are of course many ways to charge something as an amulet. Rather than give you a single ritual to use in this case, I am going to challenge you to create your own. To help you along, I am going to list just a few methods that relate to the three levels of Sorcery. You can use them separately or string together at least three in a ritual so that all three levels are represented:

Level One Empyrian/Divine/Causal methods usually focus on prayer and invocation. At this high level of work we are not talking about specific deities of protection like the God Horus, but the invocation of the *Divine itself.* Align your awareness with this level by performing the Seal of Centering and the Invocation to the Bornless

One, then *command* the object to protect its holder from harm. By your word it shall be done.

Level Two methods involve either conjuring specific spiritual powers or applying energy directly to the object. In the case of the former, you would continue to hold your divine mind from above and pray or invoke a spiritual power, such as the Archangel Michael or the Goddess Hekate, to lay their hands upon the amulet and lend it its power. Going even lower in the spectrum of this level, you could ask a nature spirit or shade of a deceased loved one to enter the object and act as protector. There are some who see this as trapping the spirit, but I can assure you that they do not experience space and time the way that we do, and there will be many spirits who jump at the opportunity to work in this way.

To apply energy directly to the amulet you can pore breathe the specific energy that you want to work with, such as the element fire, or the planet Mars, and then breathe it into the amulet. To do this, you literally breathe upon it, which is how most Tibetans consecrate their ritual implements and amulets. You can of course also find a source of power and leave the object there for a specified time to accumulate force. For instance, burying an object inside a sacred mound or exposing it to moonlight for a full cycle will charge it indirectly. You should still consecrate it verbally, so that this power is patterned to work the way you wish it to.

Level Three is of course present in the object itself, but there are other ways to bolster its magick on this level. The application of holy oil or Abramelin oil, as well as condition oils like Fiery Wall of Protection and Reversing Oil, act as an added boost. Some magicians apply fluid from their own body as a way to add power. Spitting in mojo bags is a traditional way of doing this. Sweat from the hands accumulated during prayer is another. The most powerful of these is the combined sexual fluids from an act of sex magick dedicated to the rite. Nineteenth-century African-American magus Paschal Beverly Randolph used this method to charge scrying mirrors that he sold through the mail. You can also suspend the amulet over the smoke from burning incense while you perform your invocations, infusing it materially with the herbal power from the incense.

When working with clients, they sometimes provide me with a piece of jewelry to charge as an amulet for them. If not, then I usually make them either a paper talisman or an amulet. The act of construction is part of the consecration itself. Paper seals are usually drawn on paper that has never been used for anything else and is of sturdy stock. Ceremonial magicians favor parchment and Rootworkers favor torn pieces of brown grocery bags. To me, it doesn't make much difference as long as it's thick. I also use a special ink such as dragon's blood ink.

One of the popular and famous charms is the Abracadabra Charm. The most accepted etymology of the word is that it comes from the Aramaic word *avra kehdabra,* which means, "I create as I speak." Another possibility is that it comes from a different Aramaic phrase: *abhadda kedhabhra* meaning "disappear like this word." It is this last meaning that lends itself best to its use as a written amulet.

There are many famous amulets that can be made on paper such as the Abracadabra Charm and the Sator Square. Sticking with the planetary workings presented throughout this book I would like to present two seals that arose during planetary workings with my artist Matthew Brownlee. The seals all appeared to him after I invoked the spirit of each planet to generate new and potent seals that would channel the power of the planet into material work. The Venus seal can be found in the chapter on love, but here we deal with the two planets that are used mostly in magickal security: Mars and Saturn (on the next page).

Just as we used Jupiter and Mercury to deliver a one-two punch to our financial issues, Mars and Saturn have been used together for protection in many old spells and Grimoires, including the seal of Solomon from the Goetia. Think of Saturn as a lasso or chain with which you bind up hostile forces and Mars as the weapon by which

Mars (left) and Saturn (right) Seals

you slay them or drive them back. You can use the two seals above separately or in conjunction on a single amulet.

The Conjure Hand is also known as a mojo bag or gris-gris bag. The word *gris-gris* means gray-gray and indicates that the bag has a combination of white and black magick at work in it. The number of ingredients should be an odd number—three, seven, and nine being the most common. You should avoid bags with more than thirteen ingredients.

For mojo hands, there is a wide array of herbal, mineral, and zoological material that you can combine. Asafoetida drives away disease, curses, and pretty much anything else that smells it. Devil's shoestrings bind up evil spirits. Agar-agar helps make you invisible. Eucalyptus reverses harm back upon the sender. Citronella keeps away evil, as well as mosquitos.

One of my favorite combinations is the Devil's Hand: nine pieces of Devil's shoestring to bind up the evil, a Devil Nut to scare it off, and some asafoetida, which is also called Devil's dung, to drive it away. Place it all in a black bag.

For reversing harm, I recommend eucalyptus leaves, salt, and crab shells carried in a red bag. To break up bad conditions, use salt, pepper, sulfur, and lemongrass carried in a red flannel bag. Mugwort, comfrey leaves, and fennel will keep you safe during travel, warding off not only harmful spirits, but the law as well.

Shields

Shields require no equipment other than your own will and imagination, and thus are the first line of defense when you feel attacked. Shields can be helpful not only against occult dangers, but also in psychological attacks from annoying coworkers, overzealous salespeople, brutal bosses, and any other disgruntled people that you may encounter. A police officer that tried the shielding techniques from my last book actually credited his shield with fending off a physical attack.

To create a shield, begin by performing the Pillar and Elements practice. Because this is a psychic technique that will often be used in public there is no need for words. Simply perform the practice and balance the elements along the pillar. With practice this will only take a few moments.

As you inhale, feel the power from above and from below flow into you. As you exhale, feel that energy move throughout your body, impregnating every cell of your body with power. Make a fist with your left hand and place it over your heart. Cover it with your right hand and apply about five pounds of pressure. As you inhale, feel the power gather at your heart, attracted there by the pressure and your focused will. See a small, grey egg shape gather at your heart. Release the pressure on your chest and feel the egg grow larger, passing through your skin, and stopping just at the point that it is roughly one to two feet away from your physical body. Imagine that the surface of this egg is impenetrable and that all malign forces will be unable to break its barriers.

After the image has been strongly conjured in the mind and you *know* that the shield is there, simply turn your attention away from it and go about your business. Generally the effects of the shield will wear off in a few hours unless continually fed with imagination and will. If you desire to dissolve the shield before then, simply inhale deeply, then exhale and see the shield dissolve into space.

There are several variants on this technique and ways to alter the shield to create different effects. For instance, in some cases rather than protect directly, it may be desirable to confuse or throw your enemies off-kilter. In this case, make the shield the same way, but instead of seeing the shield as grey, visualize its surface as swirling colors, like when sunlight hits oil on water. I have gotten more letters about people having success with this technique than almost anything else in my previous book. It's a great way to protect yourself from things that are not direct psychic attacks.

You can also generate a shield from one of the elemental centers along the pillar. Simply pore breathe that element and fill your whole body with it. Then, let it expand around you, encompassing you in blazing fire, rushing water, and so on. There is a Tibetan technique for creating the Sems-khor, or mind circle, that uses concentric circles of the elements. Just outside of the body is a circle of energy made from Tibetan Vajras. Outside of that is a circle of tornado-strength wind. Outside of that is a moat of rushing water, outside of that a circle of burning flame, and finally a circle of falling rocks and weapons. All of this is visualized by the meditator as a preliminary. I have oaths against revealing specific mantras and gestures associated with this practice, but a skilled Sorcerer who works with the elements will be able to create a good approximation of this powerful shield.

Use your shields judiciously. Leaving a shield up all the time will tend to cut you off from people, and even those who mean you nothing but good may find that you seem distant or unapproachable. Using confusion or elemental shields can cause even stranger reactions. Use them only when you feel that you need them.

PROTECTION FOR THE HOME

A Sorcerer's home should be a refuge, a place where the amulets can come off and you can let down your shields. Unfortunately, if not well fortified, the home can be the worst place for a Sorcerer to let their guard down. If an attacker lacks a good personal item such as hair or clothing to use as a magickal link, the cunning Sorcerer will usually target the home and use it as a giant magickal link instead. Apart from attacks, the home of a magician is the site of many rituals that will attract all kinds of varied spirits and forces. Contrary to popular occult teachings, spirits and forces are not instantly and permanently shut off when the circle is closed or a banishing ritual done. Nor should they be. A Sorcerer's home should be a house of the spirits, where not only can they be conjured and questioned, but also they can approach you in return. This is how a relationship with the intelligences and spirits is built, and we should not mistake the instructions for protecting the home below as instructions for shutting off all contact with the other worlds, powers, and denizens. We should, however, have some defense set up to repel forces that are hostile or draining to us, that may get snared into our home by our magickal actions.

Beating the Bounds

The practice of banishing by shaking and slapping weapons is common all over the world. Patagonians used to banish the demons that they believed caused smallpox by slashing at the air with swords. Inuit young women drive away evil by stabbing under their beds and at deerskins with knives. In Russia, Wotyak girls beat every corner of their house and yard with sticks split into nine pieces on the last day of the year to drive Satan out. In Australia, Aborigines banish an area by beating the ground with the stuffed tail of a kangaroo.

A practice I learned from a bishop of the Old Catholic Church that I have found useful is a ritual called "beating the bounds." Every year in England, usually on Ascension Day, parishes would have a procession of young men and boys strip willow branches and walk the perimeter of the parish, beating the ground to reinforce and remind people of the boundary lines. Obviously the furious beating of the ground sends a strong message in the spiritual world as well as to the boundary of the consecrated ground. The practice is believed to originate in the ancient Roman celebration Terminalia, a festival celebrated on February 23rd in honor of Terminus, the god of borders. Every year in February I beat the bounds around my own property line with a willow branch and make an invocation to Terminus.

INVOCATION OF TERMINUS

Apart from beating the bounds, it is good to erect at least one ritual marker at the border of your property. In the modern day, often our boundaries are marked for us with fences, or even walls if we live in an apartment. Still, a stone marker that is dedicated to Terminus serves as an excellent marker. Whether or not you beat the bounds on February 23rd, you can still make an offering of wine and honey on this stone and offer the following praise to Terminus, which is inspired by a traditional hymn from Ovid's *Fasti*. The invocation can be repeated any time that you feel your borders are under siege, be it from magick or just annoying neighbors.

> You who set bounds to peoples, cities, great kingdoms:
> Without you every field would be disputed.
> You curry no favour: you aren't bribed with gold
> Guarding the land entrusted to you in good faith.
> Stay there, in the place where you've been put,
> And yield not an inch to your neighbor's prayers,
> And whether they beat you with swords, or ploughshares,
> Call out: "This is your place, and that is his!"
> So it is, so it is, so it is.

Real Sorcery

CLEANSING

If we are already under attack, it's important to cleanse out any hostile energies, spirits, or forces before we use the previous protection procedures. If we don't cleanse first, we run the risk of sealing in what we are trying to protect ourselves from. The best way to cleanse oneself if already under attack is the same way that you would cleanse yourself from regular dirt: take a bath.

Spiritual baths are one of the oldest strata of magickal practice on this planet. From time immemorial sacred baths have been believed to clean far more than just the body, and the purity of water used in conjunction with certain herbs, minerals, and oils can yield very potent results. We see evidence of sacred baths mentioned as far back as the Sumerian Hymn to Nanna, and see their practice reflected everywhere today from the Christian baptism to the health spa. All over the world are places of power dedicated to magickal bathing: Varanasi's ghats on the Ganga river, Haiti's waterfalls of Saut-d'Eau, and Glastonbury, England's pool in King Arthur's courtyard.

The first consideration when putting together a bath ritual is the water. Traditionally you would use water from a natural source, such as a spring, lake, or water collected during rainstorms. If you live near a sacred spring or river, that is ideal as a source of water, but the general idea is that the more natural the source of the water, the better. That said, I will admit that most of the time I end up using tap water and suspect most of my clients do as well. It is far better to use tap water than not to take the bath at all!

After you have settled on the water to be used, you need to know what you are adding to the bath. Formulas typically call for three or more ingredients, usually odd numbers. These ingredients can be mineral, herbal, or zoological. There are traditional bathing formulas for everything from drawing money and love, to influencing those around you, to repelling jinxes and negativity. It is this last category that we are concerned with here.

My favorite protection formula is a bath of oak bark, cinnamon, and pine needles, brewed in the water like a tea. If you want to make something out of stuff that you probably already have in the kitchen, you can mix salt, ammonia, and vinegar. The salt and vinegar can be equal parts of about a half a cup or so, but the ammonia should only be a tablespoon. Ammonia is considered such a strong cleaner that if more is used it will remove not only negative influences, but positive and neutral ones as well.

During the bath, there is often the reading of a spell or prayer. For instance, in Hoodoo, and also in Solomonic magick, certain psalms would be read during the bath such as Psalm 23 for protection and Psalm 51 for purification. A Pagan might do well to recite one of the protection incantations from the Magickal Papyri. The Invocation of the Bornless One will make an excellent prayer for this as it was originally an exorcism.

In a protection bath you should wash yourself from the head downward. As you wash yourself, you can also conjure the purifying column from above, as per the Pillar and Elements exercise. As the herb-infused water washes you on the physical plane of Level Three, the energy from the pillar can run through you, flushing out impure energies of Level Two into the water that pools at your feet. The invocation will cleanse you on the divine/causal plane of Level One, giving you a complete cleansing on all levels of body, energy, and mind.

Cleansing Homes and Objects

To clean out a house you can use the banishing ritual from the first part of the book or a ritual such as the LBRP or Star Ruby as a start. This will push a lot of negativity and hostile energy or entities out, but the effect is temporary. As with the bath and the making of amulets, we should strive for a three-level solution to the problem.

Again, we should meditate, invoke, and pray to the highest powers of Level One. We should further invoke specific cleansing deities and angels from the realm of Level Two, as well as channeling power directly through our bodies by the means of breath and will. Level Three should be represented in terms of washes and incense.

The wash works for your home in the same way that your bath does for your body. Washes are a very old and traditional part of magick especially prevalent in African magickal traditions. There are washes to serve every magickal end: from stopping gossip, to drawing trade to brothels, to making peace, but we are concerned here only with those washes that are used in magickal cleansing and protection.

A floor wash to repel harm is applied from the rear of the house toward the front door and out, as if you were gathering up the unwanted influence and pushing it out through the door. A floor wash for attracting is done exactly the opposite and moves from the front door toward the rear of the house. If your house or building has many floors, start from above and work down to repel, and the opposite to attract. If your house is carpeted, you can mix up a batch of the wash in a spray bottle and use it to spray the carpet, or if you are more traditional, you can use a feather or an aspergillum to sprinkle the wash onto the carpet. The general pattern of either back to front or front to back should be followed whichever method you use, and it will be necessary to map out your path through the house before you begin.

As with the bath, the floor wash is ideally made with water gathered from a natural source like a river, spring, or collected rainwater. Water from the tap will do in a pinch, but water from a natural source is traditional and should be used if you can get it. A relatively small number of ingredients is added to a gallon or more of water and prayed over fervently. If you don't want to add the ingredients directly because of the chance of making a mess, you can often brew them into a tea (as described) and add that to the water.

My favorite recipe to clear away malefica is pine needles, saltpeter, and your own urine collected in complete silence first thing in the morning. As with ammonia, only a small amount is used. A recipe from a Santera teacher of mine is powdered eggshells, oak bark, and lemongrass. To wash away powers that are causing tension between people in a home or at an office, use sugar, lavender, and rose water.

There is no more prevalent and archetypal aspect to magickal ritual than the burning of incense. Nearly every culture on earth recognizes the spiritual power that certain herbs, resins, and woods have when burnt. By imbuing the material substance with our aspirations and desires, then burning it, it moves from the material to the intangible, and finally over into the spiritual dimension where our prayers are heard.

You can burn incense in a stationary holder, but if you are using it in a ceremony of cleansing or banishing you should use a censor or something that you can carry around easily. The pattern of smoking with incense is the same as washing: back to front and out the door to expel, front to back to attract.

Incense recipes abound, and you should feel free to experiment during calm times with different formulas. When you are in dire need of defense or when someone else is relying on you is not the time to try out something new, so be sure to pick out a few successful recipes before you need them.

A great general cleansing and sanctifying incense is a combination of frankincense, myrrh, and dragon's blood. For reversing harm you might try mullein, sage, and rue.

A wonderful recipe for calming poltergeists and other meddling or noisy ghosts is camphor, mint, and pine.

Washes can be said to represent the two feminine elements: water (the water for the wash) and earth (the herbs, minerals, and other ingredients in the wash). Incense represents the male elements: air (the smoke) and fire (the burning). The combination of incense and wash is a very comprehensive way to cleanse an environment or remove negative energy from an object. If you are using the wash on an object instead of a room, you can wash the item from top to bottom. Then hold the item over burning incense and allow the smoke to rise up and around the object, cleansing away whatever the wash did not.

You can coordinate the various elements of the physical forms given previously with the elemental energies within your body from the Pillar and Elements practice. In fact, there is a method taught to me by a Tibetan Sorcerer that uses elemental energy to cleanse an object directly. First, channel the energy of fire and visualize the object engulfed in a fire that burns away all impurities. Then visualize a gust of air extinguishing the fire and leaving all the impurities as ash. Next, visualize a torrent of water that washes away the ash and leaves nothing but the pure and pristine object behind. The element of earth is represented by the object itself. This method is used to purify offerings to spirits as well as ritual items.

COUNTER MAGICK

Remember what I said at the beginning of the chapter about the two main types of danger: physical and occult. Most of what I wrote about in this chapter is quite effective against occult dangers from spirits or magickal attacks. Regular magickal defensive practice is also good at diminishing physical accidents and can even be helpful in avoiding physical attacks. If, however, you are in a dire situation where someone is looking to harm or kill you physically, I would not rely upon purely protective measures for my defense. Although such situations are hopefully rare, they do happen, so our strategy would be incomplete if we did not cover some methods of dealing with these sorts of grim scenarios.

When confronted with an enemy who either is threatening physical violence or is going to persist in magickal attacks until one of them finally gets through your defenses, it is probably going to be necessary to take a more active role in defense than just the passive means we have discussed thus far. To this end, there are four main methods that can be used: to bind, confuse, expel, and counterattack. As a matter of policy, I discuss direct counterattacks aimed at harming your attacker only with personal students. It is not something I feel comfortable putting in a book such as this, and besides, it should always be a last resort. The first three modes should more than suffice even in deadly situations.

Bindings

Bindings are used to stop someone from doing a particular thing or to heavily influence someone toward doing something, in our case leaving us and our loved ones or clients alone. Obviously the information in the chapter on influencing and persuasion magick is all applicable here. You should be able to make a good binding spell out of the information provided there, but just in case, here is an effective method:

Make or purchase a doll that represents your target. I like dolls with hollow bodies that can be stuffed with binding herbs such as mullein, licorice, calamus, or even items like graveyard dirt or lead. If you can obtain a personal item from the target, make sure to include that into the doll. Mark the sign of Saturn on the chest and head of the doll.

Baptize the doll in the name of the target. To do this, make a cross over the doll with the gesture of benediction. When you make the vertical arm of the cross say: *In the name of great Saturnus.* When making the horizontal arm say: *I name thee (insert name of target).*

Take the doll in your left hand and wrap it in black bindings or chain. Tie it hand and foot. As you do this, you should be channeling the energy of the planet Saturn and praying the following:

By Saturnus I bind thy spirit
By Agiel I bind thy intellect
By Zazel I bind thy body

Thrice bound and thrice confounded art thou
Unable to cause harm or mischief
Until I release thee from thy bonds.

You can then keep the doll in a box or even bury the doll in the grave of a soldier, asking him to watch over the prisoner until you return. Whether or not you ever return to release the binding is up to you. If you do, simply untie the doll and toss it all into a river so that it gets out of your life for good.

Confusion

When binding is not possible, rites of confusion are another way to remove an enemy working against you without bringing him or her into direct harm. Some see this as a type of jinx in and of itself, but confusion spells have been used in Hoodoo and Witchcraft as protection for many, many years. When faced with an obsessive enemy that will not give up after protection and reversal rites have been worked, a bit of confusion can be a tame but effective way to deal with an enemy.

A simple confusion spell can be accomplished by the laying of confusion power where the target will come into contact with it. Confusion powder is made with poppy seeds, twitch grass, and black mustard seeds added to a powder base like talcum. Some people color their powders, and if you do, the appropriate color would be red. If you want to cause arguments and infighting as well as confusion amongst your enemies, add in black and red pepper. The same recipe could be used to make not only a powder but also an oil or incense to be used in a similar way to the influencing spells.

Expelling

The last type of counter magick that I want to cover is that of expelling, more commonly known in Rootworking as "hot-footing." This type of magick is aimed at getting a person to leave your environment totally. Usually you are expelling them either from a home, from a job, or from a town. As with confusion spells, this is most often accomplished by use of a powder as the Level Three. To this are added fiery energy from Level Two and invocations for divine protection on Level One.

Generally speaking, anything hot or stinging can be used in hot foot powder. My favorite recipe for the powder is red and black pepper, crushed hornets or red ants, sulfur, poppy seeds, and Witch's salt (salt that has been blackened with soot). This powder is used in a similar way as the others and is particularly potent if it can be "sent through the foot" by having the target walk on it or putting it in their shoes. One of my favorite ways to use this is to sprinkle it on the doorstep or office of the target, then drop a little bit at each crossroads leading out of town, praying for the person to move each time you drop it.

If you can't get close enough to a target to lay a powder, you can take a link to the person and bind it up in red cord. Soak it in hot foot oil and roll it in hot foot powder. Baptize it as you did the doll above, but instead of Saturn, call upon the powers of Mars. You could then toss it into a river to carry it away, or, if you are like me and enjoy a modern touch to your magick, mail it away to a foreign country. There is a mental hospital in Calcutta that has gotten strange packages from me once or twice. You can invoke the following as you send it off:

By the fivefold power of Mars I cast
Expel thee from my sphere
By Graphiel thou art defeated
By Bartzabel thou art driven out
Hekas Hekas Este Bebeloi
Away, Away, ye profane!

THE STRATEGY OVERVIEW

Your first line of defense is your regular practice as outlined in the first part of the book. To this you can add the short-term employment of shields when you feel you need them, as well as an amulet or two for regular use.

If you feel that you are faced with a specific danger, first use divination techniques to determine what it might be, and then respond accordingly. If you are the victim of an attack then you should start off by cleansing yourself with a ritual bath. Follow suit by cleansing your home, car, and office using a wash and incense ritual.

After cleansing, you should bolster your personal protection with a specific amulet and then protect your property by beating the bounds and performing an invocation to a protective power like Terminus. Finally, if the danger warrants it, you can bind, confuse, or expel your opponent.

There are many different variations that you could take on each of these steps. For instance, you could set up spirit traps and mirror amulets in the home instead of or in addition to beating the bounds. Our goal here is not to exhaust every possible method but to lay out a basic strategy to follow, with a few examples of how to fulfill the strategy. My book *Protection and Reversal Magick* will have much more detail than I can put into this chapter, but in every chapter it is the basic strategy that I hope you walk away with, not the specifics of a bunch of spells.

NEW EDITION COMMENTARY— REASONABLE PROTECTION

Have you ever seen the 1981 film *Excalibur*? It's great, but one of the odd things is that Arthur, Mordred, and all the knights wear their heavy jousting armor throughout the whole movie. They fight in it, they eat dinner in it, at one point someone has sex while wearing it.

Very unrealistic. Heavy armor like that keeps you safe, but it also weighs you down and keeps you from being able to do anything that requires a lot of dexterity. This is why in most roleplaying games, the Rogue can wear only leather armor, and the Wizard doesn't get to wear any at all.

The same thing is true of magickal defenses. If you are maxing out your banishing rituals, shields, and amulets, it will make finding and connecting to spirit allies and powers that much more difficult. We need to find a balance between protection that you would use if you knew you were under attack, and going without any protection at all. We need *reasonable* protection that meets the needs of the moment.

When you get into a car to drive to the grocery store, you hopefully wear a seat belt and drive a car with airbags. This level of protection is reasonable for driving in ordinary traffic. Yes, you can still get into an accident and get hurt. You can even get killed, but you consider it a reasonable risk. If you decide to drive in a race, the danger level goes up and so does your protection. You wear a helmet and a five-point harness. Your car has a roll cage to keep it from collapsing. Would all this keep you safer during ordinary traffic? Of course, but the protection needed on the way to the grocery store doesn't justify the hassle and expense. Understand?

My advice is to put twice as much effort into establishing spiritual authority as you do into specific protection rituals and shielding. If you are known as someone who can handle themselves magickally and call upon powerful forces when you need to, you will wind up having more effective magick than if you go for the "boy in the bubble" approach.

In times of danger and conflict, of course, you should do whatever you feel you need to. These are the times you should go all out and enjoy the confidence of a magickal fortress. If you feel you are in constant danger, and thus need this fortress-level protection all the time, you probably need to make some different life choices.

CHAPTER 9

Love and Lust

NOTE: I will be blunt. I don't like love magick aimed at influencing or binding a specific target. It's absolutely traditional, and for that reason I talked about it a good bit in the first edition of this book. Since then we have seen millions of women as well as several prominent men step forward with stories of sexual abuse and harassment. In that same time span, we have seen a once somewhat playful movement of "pick up artists" morph into the horrifying domestic terrorist threat of "incels," or involuntary celibates.

I left most of this book unchanged, simply including updates at the end of each chapter. This chapter I felt really needed to change and has been reworked entirely. The fact that spells aimed at coercing specific targets into love or sex is traditional is not a sufficient reason for practicing it now.

The novelist Nora Roberts once said, "Love and magick have a great deal in common. They enrich the soul, delight the heart. And they both take practice." She hit the nail right on the head. Whether you are alone right now and looking for love, or have been married for decades, success at love takes work and skill. Yet, more than any other topic we will cover in this book, people generally just play the cards they are dealt and give almost no thought to improving their techniques, trying the same thing over and over again. People think nothing of improving their knowledge of handling money or of gaining new skills for a new hobby, but if you suggest that someone improve their skills in the arts of love, it somehow seems more daunting. People seem to want love to come effortlessly. Rather than work on the skills necessary to maintain a relationship, many couples would rather end it because "he or she was obviously not *the one*."

It is true that, if we are to find real love, we must be loved for who we are. But, before someone can fall in love with you enough to see who you really are, they need to be attracted to you, and attraction is a whole different ball of wax. Although some people may be naturally and instantly attractive, there is also an art to attraction that can be learned and mastered.

TYPES OF LOVE MAGICK

I divide love magick into two main categories: attraction and relationship magick. The bulk of this chapter will be about attraction, as that is what most classical love magick is devoted to. We will cover relationship magick at the end of the chapter.

Attraction magick is further divided into two types of workings:

1. Those that target a specific person.

2. Those that draw unknown people who would naturally be attracted to you.

Most ancient love magick is devoted to the former. Incantations for forcing named women to fall in love with you and philters fed to men to arouse lust and faithfulness are common in medieval spell books, Egyptian papyri, and even in Indian alchemical texts. There is also no shortage of spells aimed at members of the same sex. One of the examples we have record of is by a monk hoping to bind the love of another monk.

Most modern love magick is devoted to the latter purpose, feeling that it is better to allow the magick to guide you than to directly influence someone's will. This is a much better idea in general.

There is nothing wrong with attempting to win the love of a girl that you are smitten with. Nothing wrong with pursuing a man who initially shows no interest. Some of the world's greatest love stories have arisen from such endeavors. There is a difference however between initial disinterest and a firm "No." A competent Sorcerer should not let attraction become obsession. Cases of unrequited love should just be accepted as a dead issue.

Using magick to attract a mate who would naturally be attracted to you can be a useful alternative, but I am skeptical of turning my life's path over to the spirits or trusting magick to guide my life. Being a Sorcerer, Sorceress, or Sorcerix means making decisions for yourself and taking responsibility for those decisions. Some people like to make a list of features and qualities that they would like their potential lover to have. Unfortunately, even when these types of spells get fulfilled to the letter, the reality often falls short. In the end, what makes us attracted to someone and attractive to others is not just a bunch of qualities that we can rattle off like a grocery list.

We need ultimately to be the ones who decide whom we pursue as potential lovers, but we also need to be open to magick and providence to provide opportunities that we may not see if we are too fixated on a specific person, or a specific type.

INNER LOVE MAGICK

Obviously, some love magick is a subset of influence and persuasion magick. Be sure that you understand that chapter thoroughly because we will be building upon some of the themes presented in that chapter here, focusing on indirect influence. You will remember that indirect influence is work that you do upon yourself that makes you a more influential person overall, as opposed to direct influence, where you are working directly upon the mind of another person. Indirect influence, or inner attractiveness in this case, is vital for love magick. People who are looking for a love spell to make the girl or boy of their dreams turn up on their doorstep while they remain a hapless schlump are just fooling themselves. As we have pointed out many times so far: magick doesn't work that way.

BOOSTING ATTRACTIVE QUALITIES

The biggest mental stumbling block that people have in attraction magick is the idea that they are somehow not good-looking enough to attract the kind of people that they desire. I am not going to lie to you or feed you some bull about society's fascist standards of beauty. Some people are just blessed with good looks. Some people are stunningly beautiful. Many of us are not. But that doesn't matter.

Physical attractiveness only gets your foot in the door; it doesn't keep you inside. Good humor, sultriness, cockiness, a sharp wit—any one of these qualities can be cultivated so that they more than compensate for ways in which your own beauty and the standards of beauty that society currently subscribes to diverge.

That is not to say that you shouldn't make the most of your physical appearance. If you are looking for a lover, or even just looking to put a bit of fire back into your existing relationship, you should always make sure that you are groomed well and that you are wearing clothes that flatter your body type. If you can afford it, invest in a stylist and someone to advise you on what types of clothes look good on your body type. If not, pay attention to television shows like *What Not to Wear* and read books about style. If you are unhappy with your body type, get to the gym and build some muscle, or try a nutritionist-approved diet. With a little effort and motivation, you can increase your physical attractiveness and your confidence in a short amount of time. If you do it, it will pay off not only in love, but in other relationships as well. If, however, you feel like you continue to look like an unmade bed, then it's going to be that much harder to overcome it with magick. *Help the magick help you.*

My advice is to make sure you do the best you can with qualities across the board, but focus in on boosting your best and most attractive qualities. If you don't know what these are, ask someone who knows you well. If you are funny, let your humor be the star of the show. Same if you are very caring or charming or adventurous or whatever. Lead with your strength. If you have a tendency to talk too much about yourself (my personal poison . . .), work on that. If you come off as awkward or too forward, find ways to work on that as well.

Once you figure out what qualities you need to shore up and what strength you want to lead with, it's time to throw some magick into the mix.

SUMMONING OF THE SEDUCER

Sound the seed syllable of Venus: η (the Greek vowel eta, which is pronounced *eh* as in "bet"). The pitch should start high and end low. In this case, you should feel that the force begins to flow from the planet toward the sigil in front of you at the high pitch, and then into your body as the pitch deepens.

After the utterance of the seed syllable, invoke the following:

Oh mother of love
Oh maiden of grace
I utter the sacred seed sound,
And offer it in praise
Echo it back upon me
And bestow upon me your boon
Of charm and appeal
Magnetize my words

And fascinate my gaze
That all shall fall before me
In devotion and desire
By the power of η (eh)
By the grace of IAO
Grow forth and witness!

At the conclusion of the invocation, use the pore breathing technique to absorb the energies of Venus. See hooked rays of light radiating from your heart that enter and draw toward you all that you find desirable.

Open your eyes and anoint your head, throat, chest, and hands with attraction oil or similar condition oil to seal the invocation into the physical plane.

This invocation has an important second part. After performing this invocation, you should go out into the world and start flirting. Flirt with anyone and everyone that you find attractive. It could be the guy at the office, the barista at the coffee shop, whoever, just flirt. When you do so, remember the lessons on influence from chapter six.

Meditate on Rejection

After you get used to flirting a bit, start asking for phone numbers or emails. My recommendation is that the more afraid you are of doing this, the more you need to do it. Not so that you can be sure to succeed, but so that you can be sure to *get rejected*. You read that right, I want you to get rejected. The only way that I know of to conquer the fear of rejection is to face it. You will be in the headspace created by the Venusian Seducer ritual and you will experience rejection in that state.

Meditate on it. Just as in meditation, thoughts arise in the mind-stream, then dissipate without really affecting the nature of mind;

rejection can and will happen without really affecting you in any way. Every fighter knows what it is like to lose a fight, and it's only by doing so that they conquer their fear of loss. You must conquer your fear of rejection in the same way.

Tap into the energy of the Venusian Seduction invocation and boldly approach your target or group of targets within two minutes of deciding to do so. Two minutes is enough time to get your thoughts together, but not enough time for your doubts to overtake you.

Behaviors in Others

When you are looking for love it's not always easy to know if someone is interested in you or not. This is where looking for so-called "IOIs" or "Indicators of Interest" come in. Remember that most peoples' thoughts and behaviors are mechanistic and preprogrammed. Most people tend to do the same things when they are attracted to someone. Here are some helpful signs.

- Looking directly into your eyes.

- Women playing with their hair or picking at their skin.

- Men checking their clothes and grooming.

- Laughing at everything you say, even your dumbest jokes.

- Moving to face you while talking.

- Touching you in the course of conversing.

- Unprovoked fiddling with clothing and jewelry.

- Leaning in while talking.

- A sense of jealousy when mentioning another person.

If you are having trouble reading or noticing someone's behavior, you can test for indicators of interest by performing an interest test. You can for instance deliberately drop a conversation, and if your target quickly jumps to fill the silence with a question aimed at keeping the conversation going, that is a good indicator of interest. If you walk over to an area of a room where there are several chairs and a couch and he or she sits next to you on the couch as opposed to a chair, that's a good one too. One of my favorites is to pick up my coat or gloves, and see if my target asks if I am getting ready to leave.

If you can observe at least three of these behaviors in your target, it's a good bet that you can lean in and perhaps establish physical contact by appropriately touching their arm or leg and go deeper into the dance.

Just remember that even if all the indicators of interest are there, a "No" is still a "No." If they are not interested, it doesn't say anything about you, or them, other than they aren't looking at you like that.

VENUSIAN TALISMANS

Just as you can charge all kinds of things as protection amulets, you can do the same for Venusian talismans. All kinds of things have been said to bring luck in love, from sachets of lavender, damiana, and cardamom worn between the breasts, to complex symbols engraved on copper disks. My all-time favorite for men has to be the raccoon penis bone, or "C." Though many mammals possess a baculum, or bone in their penis, the raccoon's is abnormally large considering the size of the animal. It is almost the size of a bear's and is therefore valued in love spells.

The talisman that I want to share is one that appeared during an invocation of Kedemel, the spirit of Venus. This is one of a group of seven seals; the others will remain secret until the omens are right to reveal them. The seal bestows all the influential powers of Venus on the wearer, but more importantly draws people to you with whom you would naturally be compatible. This is true in not only matters of love, but all other matters as well. It is to be inscribed on a disk of copper, on a Friday at the hour of Venus.

Venus Seal

You should consecrate the talisman outside in the early morning when Venus, the morning star, is just beginning to rise in the sky. Place the talisman on an altar so that the talisman is just below your view of the rising planet, or at least where you know the planet to be.

Perform the rending of space and sound the seed syllable of Venus, "*eh*." Then proceed with the following invocation:

In the name of IAO
By the power of Hagiel
I call upon thee, Kedemel
Oh thou spirit of Venusian grace
Behold this seal and remember!
Let shine upon it the rays of Aphrodite
That it may summon and ensnare
Those whom its wearer desires
That it may arouse friendship
That it may arouse trust
That it may arouse love
That it may arouse lust
In all who come within its presence
In the name of IAO, the most high
So it shall be.

You can wear the talisman under your clothes or carry it in your wallet. You should avoid letting other people see the talisman, especially those you are attempting to influence.

A Full Moon Seduction Ritual

Just as Jupiter is not the only planet used in financial magick, Venus is not the only planet that is useful in love magick. The moon as the planet of intuition and emotion makes it a most excellent planet for seduction and love magick. The following ritual is meant to be targeted on someone that you have already met, but have not yet "sealed the deal" with.

Purchase or make yourself a red figurine candle appropriate to the gender of the target. Write the target's name on the back of the candle and baptize it in that name so that it represents the target. If you have an object link to the target, you can lay it on an altar or table that is basking in the light of the full moon. This is where you will do the spell. It is best if the moon is bright enough to do the spell with no other lights on. It is also best performed when you think that the target might be asleep.

Hold the red figure candle in your hands and call your target's name three times out into the night. Turn your attention to the candle now and use your fascination gaze to empower it as a true representative of your sleeping target. Take an appropriate condition oil and begin to work it into the candle. The trick here is that rather than rubbing it away from you or toward you, you will be working the oil into the candle as you would rub oil onto a lover's body. Whisper fantasies to it. If these are fantasies that you know the target has, then they will be even more effective. Tell it the things you are going to do, and what you want it to do to you. Enflame yourself with passion as you do this.

When you are finished, place the candle on top of the object link. Invoke the following, adjusting the invocation to the target's pronouns as necessary:

Oh Luna
Silvery goddess of gravity and grace
Take hold of the mind of [say your target's name]
And fill her (or his or their) thoughts with fervor
Let passion haunt her dreams
Let infatuation drive her days
Let fancy take fill
And lust unfold
Let a tide of desire
Sweep her swiftly toward me
And a flame of yearning
Make her melt before me
So that only my touch
Can soothe her burning
[Here, whisper the name of the target.]
Hear me, Hear me

Light the wick at the head of the candle and let it burn all the way down, melting right onto the material link, and into his or her thoughts.

While this is an act of direct influence and thus targeted love magick, it can easily be adapted to attract someone to you that would melt at your touch. Also, the level of influence it bestows is not a level that I would consider coercive or aggressive. Consider it the magickal equivalent of finding out some things that your potential lover likes and dislikes to help you put your best foot forward.

MARRIAGE, LOVE, AND THE LONG HAUL

If you can see how close you are to the end of this chapter, you might be asking why so much of this chapter has been about seduction, attraction, and sex rather than romance, marriage, and long-term commitment. Do I think the former is more important and fulfilling than the latter? No, certainly not. It's just that Sorcery is not what leads you into real love and long-term commitment. At least it shouldn't.

Sorcery can start you off on the path for sure, but ultimately it should be the genuine connection between two people that leads them into a committed relationship. It has been said that it is our features that make us attractive, but our flaws that make us loveable, therefore it is only when we reveal ourselves fully to one another that a good relationship is made. Whatever courage you needed to summon to overcome your fear of rejection is going to need to be summoned constantly if you hope to reveal yourself in this manner.

That said, there are some tips and rituals that can help facilitate the work of a marriage or serious relationship. Looking at history, the most common of these are spells to keep a husband or wife from cheating. Some are as simple as feeding your mate a philter of your sexual fluids to keep them from straying. Some are quite extreme and involve severe punishments for a cheating spouse, such as some Mexican novenas to Santísima Muerte, a skeletal form of the Virgin Mary representing death, that seek to keep a man "restless and bothered" and actually threaten the life of a cheating husband who does not return. This is nothing new, of course. Even in the book of Numbers in the Old Testament, we have a description of a ritual whereby a wife suspected of cheating is brought into the Tabernacle with her head uncovered (to expose her to the Lord) and made to drink a cursed water. If she is innocent, the Lord is said to protect her from the curse. If not, then she dies.

I actually loathe all such rituals and don't recommend them. Bindings and curses have their place—I have used them both—but if your significant other is going to cheat, then it's indicative of a deeper problem that you need to deal with using measures other than influencing and cursing. Otherwise, it's better to just let it go. I mention these spells only because they are traditional, and to completely ignore them is to do a disservice to the tradition. Just because it's traditional in magick, however, does not mean it's a good idea.

That said, there is nothing at all wrong with placing a blessing upon a union. This is one of the functions of the marriage ceremony itself. Even if you are married, it is good to update and refresh your blessings with a little Sorcery.

You can, for instance, charge your wedding rings as talismans of love, passing them through an incense of myrrh and frankincense, calling upon the highest spiritual powers to lay their hands upon your union and bless it. I like the following invocation:

Omnia in Duos, Duos in Unum,
(All in two, two in one)
Gloria Patri et Matri
(Glory to the Father and Mother)
Et Filio, et Filiae
(to the Son and Daughter)
Et Amor Sanctus
(to the sacred love)
Ute rat, est erit
(which was and shall be)
In Secula Seculorem
(world without end)
Omnia in Duos, Duos in Unum
(All in two, two in one)
In Nominae IAO

To this, you can add a personal request like the following:

Bless this union with devotion and discretion.
With Love and loyalty
With Happiness and Home.

As certain situations arise within the relationship, you can use many of the techniques throughout this book to help. The section on financial magick will help keep the financial problems away, the number one cause of divorce. If danger threatens the home, you can rely upon the strategies for protection to see you through.

Apart from money, the most common problem in long-term relationships is a slowdown in sexual relations. Remember the lessons in seduction above. They do not hold only for people that you just met. Use some of the spells to stir the passions of your partner, but don't forget to be attentive in the more mundane ways as well. Sometimes it is necessary to use more care, effort, and cunning into getting our spouse into bed after years of marriage than it did when we did it the first time. Dress up for each other. Husbands: put on a suit and take her on a date like it's the first time. Wives: wear the lingerie and boots. Keep it exciting.

THE STRATEGIC REVIEW

I will repeat again that we must remember that success comes from a mixture of mundane and magickal efforts. We cannot cast a love spell and expect it to work if we continue to stay in and watch TV every night. Likewise, if we go out, but appear to be a shy, frustrated, sloppy mess, we won't get very far.

Our strategy begins with indirect love magick, working on the self. Figure out your strengths. What qualities do you possess that people have found attractive? Everyone has them. Weave these qualities into a seductive identity. Will you be a coquettish maiden or an aggressive vamp? A charming gentleman, or a cocky comedian? Figure out what works for you and develop it. Study people who display those qualities.

Update your looks. Invest in some new clothes and accessories that will make you stand out from the crowd. Sometimes an interesting-looking love talisman can act not only as a magickal charm but also as a conversation piece. I met a guy at a club once who had a necklace made with beads and seven raccoon penis bones. It looked like something a Stone Age Shaman would wear, but plenty of ladies kept asking him about it. He would tell them outright that it was a love charm and segue into a conversation about magick. A few minutes later, he had their phone numbers.

Next step is to build your confidence. Use the summoning of the seducer, then go out and flirt. Start conversations with strangers and ask for numbers. When you get shot down, meditate on the rejection. What is there to it? Nothing. It's just words. Move on to the next one. Eventually you will overcome your fear and project an aura of confidence and competence.

Now it's time to go out and meet some people whom you would like to date. Start by making yourself the Venusian talisman or a similar love charm to help draw people to you who will be receptive to your attempts. When you talk to people, watch your behavior: Don't come on too eagerly or aggressively. Keep an open face and body language. Lean back and approach from the side. Show you know your own value by displaying interest with a willingness to walk away. Always have someplace to be. If the object of your desire is in a group, talk to the group before you engage with your potential love interest. Find out how they all know each other.

Watch for signs of interest from your potential love interest. Commit the list of behaviors to memory and use the behavior tests. Do not forget to incorporate some of the conversational Sorcery from the Influence chapter. Read some of the books from people who work in the field of erotic attraction, be they exotic dancers or famous lotharios; there is nothing wrong with learning something from people that rely upon their skills for a living.

Don't talk about your job; that's boring. Be playful. Talk about spirituality. Play a few games. Tell some of your best stories. If there is a bawdy or sexual component to these stories, then all the better. Just don't drift into vulgarity or become threatening in your overtures. You need not be lewd to be titillating. Once you have a few of the indicators of interest, you can lean in and perhaps lay a hand on the arm or knee of the target. If they don't pull away, you are probably in a good position to ask for a number or even share a kiss. You should not rush this. You might get a number in fewer than ten minutes, but that doesn't mean he or she will answer when you call. Plan to spend about a half hour with someone so that you have established a solid connection.

Once you get your foot in the door, collect a few personal links and use them in temple spells like the lunar seduction spell. Continue to use your influencing and seduction skills on further dates. Here is an additional tip: instead of just going out to one place on a date, go to several in one night. Dinner should be at one place, dessert at another, with something fun in between. This is a sort of temporal trickery that gives the impression of a longer history with this person than you actually have. If they look back in their mind and see all these places where you've been and things you have done, it will be easier for you to invite them to stay the night, even if all this happened on your first date. (Remember, though, as we've discussed: "No" is always a "No.")

As time passes in your relationship, you can drop some of the pretense and flirting, and, instead, focus on opening up to your partner. Explore and fulfill their fantasies, and they will be more likely to do the same for you. Bless your relations ritually by calling upon the highest powers.

No relationship is perfect. Use individual spells and strategies to address problems as they arise, even if that means rehashing the seduction strategies. Never take anything or anyone for granted. Everything takes work and skill.

CHAPTER 10

Further Strategies

I could keep going on and on presenting new rituals spells for everything you could possibly think of, but that is not the real purpose of this book. As I mentioned in the introduction, there are plenty of spell books out there. What I want to do is provide a field guide for working with magick, not just a massive collection of every ceremony, spell, and trick that I know. Anyone can collect a group of spells, but it takes a genuine Sorcerer to know the best ways to implement them for maximum effect.

In the first part of the book, I laid out the basics of how Sorcery works and provided subtle keys and regular practices that will awaken your psycho-spiritual gifts and cultivate genuine magickal power. In the second part of the book, I laid out strategies for gathering intelligence, influencing others, increasing finances, providing protection, and finding love. These are the basic needs that magick can help fulfill for yourself and others. I would like to take a few pages now and explore some other issues, and how the strategies and knowledge we have already taught can be applied to finding a sorcerous solution.

LEGAL MATTERS

Legal trouble is one of the most common issues for which people seek magickal help. Many Sorcerers have made their name by manipulating the legal system. The famed Voodoo Queen Marie Laveau for instance is rumored to have gotten her house on Rue St. Ann when a Creole man offered her the house in exchange for getting his son an innocent verdict in a murder trial. Marie went to St. Louis Cathedral on Jackson Square and prayed all morning with three guinea peppers in her mouth. She then snuck into the courtroom and placed them under the judge's seat to influence his decision.

Working the Judge

I was taught a similar spell to the one Marie Laveau performed that uses galangal root, sometimes called "Little John to Chew" or even more commonly "Court Case Root." You pray for success in your case while chewing the root and letting the saliva accumulate in your mouth. If you can somehow gain access to the courtroom before your case, you should spit a bit of the root onto the floor where you think the judge will walk. If not, then you can use the spit like you would a powder and dress legal documents with it, or, failing that, just rub it on the furniture in the courtroom.

There are also court-case powders you can use that contain galangal. At one time, it was popular to mail an envelope with the powder in it to the judge, who would come into contact with it when opening the letter. Although you would think that in this day of anthrax scares and terrorist threats, no one would mail powders anymore, this is not the case. At the time of writing this book, I was mailed a link to a story about a court in Fayetteville where a courthouse was closed down because of a harmless white powder in an envelope. Similar stories have popped in Boston, New York, and Oakland. Unless you want to compound whatever situation drew you into court with an FBI investigation, please *do not* mail powders to anyone.

Of course, spells aimed at the judge are only one angle to work. A strategic Sorcerer will work magick on the judge, the prosecutor, the defense attorney, witnesses, and the situation itself. The judge we have covered. You can use the previous galangal spell, or any of the influencing techniques from the earlier chapter. Be specific. Get the judge's name, don't just aim it at "the judge." In the age of Google, you can find out all sorts of useful information to use in the spell, like his birthdate and possibly even a photo. Be clever and you can gather some good object links this way.

Prosecution

In most cases where magick is involved, the prosecutor is the enemy. Go back to the protection section and use the measures that you deem appropriate. Because you are probably not going to be able to completely bind or expel a prosecutor (they would just replace him with someone else), I have found confusion rites to be particularly useful.

If the prosecutor is on your side, you can use the following techniques to bolster the prosecution instead of the defense.

Defense

For your own attorney, I recommend a blessing ritual to bolster his luck. Obtain an object link and place it in a red bag with some sunflower seeds, galangal root, cascara sagrada, High John the Conqueror, lucky hand root, and the Kamea of Sol drawn on parchment. Light a yellow candle that has the sigil of the sun either etched on it or painted on the outside of the glass if you are using an encased candle. Light the candle and pass the bag over the flame while uttering the following prayer:

> HELIOS, hear my urgent plea!
> Lend me your light that my defender may shine!
> NAKHIEL, lend him your logic,

That his arguments dispel the darkness.
SORATH, lend him your sword,
That he may cut through the injustice set against me.
IO SOLAS!

Let the candle burn down and carry the bag with you to court. If you know the attorney well, you can even request that he carry it himself.

Witnesses

If there are witnesses in the case, you can again refer to the influencing and protection chapters. If the truth will hurt your case (hey, I'm not here to judge), then use a binding or expelling spell to protect yourself. If the truth will help you, then you can use a spell to help the truth come out. Get a link to the witness and hold it over an incense made from slippery elm, adder's tongue, and High John. Address the link as if you are addressing the person directly.

By Pistis you will tell the truth
By Aletheia you will tell the truth
By Themis you will tell the truth
You will honor your oath
You will tell the truth

Lady Justice

After you have affected all the individual players in the case, you should cast a spell over the case as a whole. One week before your case is to be heard, set up a small altar using an image of Justice as the central feature. You can use the Justice card from your favorite tarot deck—in fact, you can use several. Light the candles and perform the Invocation of the Bornless One, followed by the rending of space. Light an appropriate incense and appeal now to Lady Justice directly every day for the next week, using a new candle every day:

Oh THEMIS, Mighty Daughter of GAIA and URANUS
Who brought order out of chaos.
Send to me your daughter DIKE
That she may banish the demon ADIKIA
And grant me favor in my hour of need.
Oh IUSTITIA, Impartial and Fair
Hear my urgent plea!
May your balance find me absolved
And your staff find me victorious
May justice be done.
May Justice be done.

I should add that this petition works only if your case is just. If you are in the wrong, then you should purify yourself with a hyssop bath and by fasting for at least three days. Confess your guilt to the universe and ask for absolution. Then, if you truly feel that further punishment would be wrong, you can appeal to Justice. If not, then the preceding ritual will at most offer a bit of leniency.

Just remember, though, you have numerous angles to work from: the prosecution, the defense, the judge, the witnesses, and yourself. That's five different rituals. If one of them fails, the others will still assist you. That's what strategic Sorcery is all about.

Of course, do not forget the mundane aspects of winning in court. Find a good lawyer. Dress like you are at an important job interview. Prepare any remarks you are going to make. These will all do as much for you as your magick will.

HEALTH AND LONGEVITY

People in the spiritual/magickal communities often have very strong opinions on health, many of which conflict. Some insist that vegetarianism and abstinence from alcohol are necessary for spiritual growth. Others point out that Tibetan Buddhists eat meat and drink as part of their spiritual practice, and John the Baptist ate nothing but locusts. Some insist on eating only organic foods and drinking heavily filtered water to keep out toxicants. Others believe that this will make your immune system weak to the toxic elements that you are bound to encounter at some point during your life. If you are looking for a holistic and spiritual guide to complete health, you aren't going to get it here. Spiritual and magickal health disciplines like acupuncture, ayurveda, massage, and herbalism abound. They are all too complex to be dealt with in a single chapter, but all worth incorporating into your health strategy. Choose your health ideology as ye will.

I am not going to lecture you about your health much at all, in fact. You know what you should be doing and what you shouldn't be doing. If you are like me, you probably just don't do most of it. That's not okay, by any means, but a few paragraphs in a book about Sorcery are not going to make you quit smoking or start exercising an hour a day. I am just being realistic here. There are, however, a few habits that you can adopt to lead a healthier life, many of which can be helped along by methods already covered in this book.

Start with Your Doctor
The first step is to see your doctor and get a checkup. Find out if anything is wrong. Find out your ideal weight. Talk to her about exercise and vitamin regimens that other patients of hers find easy to adopt. Talk to her about how much sleep you should be getting.

Take your suggestion list from the doctor back to your temple. Make a list of steps that you can take to start adopting them. Create sigils for five habits that you want to adopt and draw them inside a pentagram. Place your own name or seal at the center of the pentagram. Perform the Invocation of the Bornless One and swear that you will adopt these five habits. Place all the sigils inside a red bag or cloth with a string attached so it can be worn about the neck.

If you are very serious about the process, you can actually add to your declaration that if you do not adopt the habits, the very spirits that are subject unto you will turn against you until you are successful. Your own Agathodaimon will then see to it that these spirits turn against you if you fail to adopt the habits. The torment will cease only once you have picked the new habit up again. If you meditate regularly, you will be able to drop and adopt habits much more easily than if you don't. This is because if you meditate you will be able to easily recognize thoughts generated by habitual patterns and separate them from your true will.

Sample Health Pentagram

Meditation

If you have been performing your regular practices diligently, you will be meditating regularly. This is a huge key to good health. Apart from the spiritual benefits of meditation, it has enormous health benefits. Various university studies have shown that people who meditate daily experience some of the following benefits:

- Lower blood pressure

- Boosted immune system

- Lowered cholesterol levels

- Reduced stress and anxiety

- Reduced depression

- Reduced irritability and moodiness

- Feelings of vitality and rejuvenation

- Increased emotional control

- Increased confidence

- Improved concentration

I was quite serious when I said that if I had to choose just one thing to practice and one thing to teach to students, it would be meditation. When I was teaching weekly meditation classes at a holistic studio a few years back, a potential student asked me how many classes they would need to attend to gain some benefit. "One," I answered. You *need* only one meditation technique. In the end, the meditation techniques are all ways of entering contemplation, not contemplation itself. Eventually the method is dropped and the mind unites with the Azoth, or, if you prefer, Spirit/Space. It is good to know various methods to accommodate various conditions and beings, but the only one that really means anything is the one that enters you into contemplation.

Elemental Healing

According to many types of traditional medicine, many of the health problems that can arise in the physical body of Level Three have a corresponding problem in the energetic body of winds and channels on Level Two. Chinese, Indian, and Tibetan traditional doctors have mapped out very detailed maps of these winds and channels and study for years to master healing them. There are, however, some more basic models that can help us with our health.

One of these models is based upon the five elements. According to Tibetan medicine, earth is the flesh and bone of the body, also said to rule the sense of smell. Water is the fluid of the body: the blood, encephalic fluid, and so on. It is said to lubricate the muscles and tendons. It is also said to rule the sense of taste. Fire controls and regulates body temperature, generates heat throughout the body, gives color to the skin, and contributes to the growth and development of the body. It is said to rule the sense of sight. Air provides the ability to move and breathe, and rules the skin and the sense of feeling. Azoth or space allows things to grow, develop, mature, and move. It rules the pores and the sense of sound.

Remember the subtle key about pore breathing the elements? This is another small technique with huge benefits if you master it. If you have a problem related to the fluids in the body, it may be related to an elemental imbalance in the subtle body. For instance, if you are asthmatic you might try pore breathing the element air over a prolonged period of time. If you have a blood disorder, you may try to pore breathe the element water. Fire for nerves, and so on. If you feel that your body has an overabundance of an element, like, say, water in the lungs, you can pore breathe the opposing element, in this case fire.

Offerings
Offerings are also profoundly important to good health. You do not really end at your skin. Every being changes almost all of its cells within seven years. You are in a constant exchange with your environment, taking things in through respiratory and digestive processes. This also happens on a spiritual level. By making offerings to spiritual guests, you pacify various forces that may be offended by the way you live and behave. These are not things that you did on purpose, but through pollution, building, driving, and so on, we can sometimes trample on spiritual powers that are invested in sites that

we disturb. A good deal of Shamanism is designed to heal these rifts. Perform the offerings frequently.

Relaxation

Relaxation is another key to psychic health. Meditation will naturally relax you, but it is sometimes useful to be able to command the body to relax at a moment's notice. This is easily done by simply going through the body part by part and commanding it to relax. If you have time, you can take a good thirty minutes and start at the toes, working your way up to the top of the head, going part by part. Most of the time this is inconvenient, so it's good to know certain key sections that hold a lot of tension in them.

Focus on the small muscles around the eyes and tell them to relax. Next are the muscles in the forehead; tell them to relax. Now your abdominal muscles. If you are tense, these tend to be the three places we carry it. Once you relax these three areas, scan the body and see if there are any others. Tell them to relax. Repeat the process ten minutes later, and again ten minutes after that. The muscles tend to retighten once your attention is moved away from them.

Healing Transference and Sacrifice

In many types of folk magick, serious cases of sickness can be transferred to animals, which are then sacrificed. In Voodoo, this is most often done with a chicken that is rubbed up and down the afflicted person's body while the sickness is lured out and into the chicken. Nepalese Shamans called Jankris do the same thing with an egg, placing it next to the afflicted part of a person's body and luring the damage out of the patient by drumming and chanting healing mantras.

You can use the egg method in self-healing. To do this, you must invoke and call down the light of spirit into your body. You can use the Invocation of the Bornless One followed by the Pillar and

Spheres exercise to do this. Establish the pillar or simply imagine that a white purifying light has descended from infinite space and entered through the crown of your head, filling your body with light, pushing physical and emotional disease out of your body as it does so. Take an egg and make a prayer to your deities. Rub the egg over yourself starting from the head and moving down the body. This gives the sickness someplace to go other than to resettle in the body.

When you are finished you should take the egg someplace and bury it with respect. Just as if you had used a live chicken, what was once a potential life has done you a service by taking your disease into itself, sacrificing itself in the process. Even though it is just an egg, you should make an offering to the spirit of this potential life and commit it to the ground with respect and where the disease can be absorbed into Mother Earth.

The subject of psychic and magickal health is quite vast. I could easily write an entire book on the subject, but for now I just want to focus on building upon the health benefits from the various techniques we have already taught. Use the health amulet and commitment ceremony to take on five new habits. Maximize the health benefits of your meditation practice. Balance the elements with pore breathing. Learn to relax, and, if necessary, use the transference technique to remove sickness from the body.

You should also take up a form of exercise that complements your Sorcery. Yoga, qigong, kung fu, and tai chi all have practices that work the physical body of Level Three as well as the subtle body of Level Two. Like I said, you know what you should be doing. So do it.

GOING PRO

There is an aspect of practice that exists all over the world, but is spoken about very little in the Western traditions of either ceremonial magick or Witchcraft: doing it professionally. I don't mean writing about it and teaching how to do it. I mean actually doing magick for money.

In fact, there seems to be strong objection to this in many quarters of the magickal community. Some object that magick should be primarily spiritual, and therefore beyond money. Others worry about being in the same league as charlatans and scam artists that milk people for thousands of dollars to remove fake curses.

Yet these same folks are clearly alright with certain aspects of magick being for sale. Few object to the idea of charging for tarot readings. Why, then, is it not alright to charge for spellwork?

I have been working as a professional Sorcerer for about seven years now and have some strong opinions on the subject myself. I would like to take the opportunity to close out our strategies by dealing with some of these objections, and to offer a strategy for professional Sorcerers out there.

First, let's deal with the spiritual bugaboo. At a recent occult convention I attended, I happened to overhear two people discussing how it's evil for anyone to even charge for magickal training, much less the performance of magick. Hopefully in the section on financial magick I dealt successfully with the notion that money is somehow *unspiritual*. It's not. It is in fact a spirit in a very real sense. If you insist that money is evil and unspiritual, you are probably never going to have very much of it.

Everything we do in this life takes time. We all have to spend a certain amount of time in our lives earning money. If we relegate magick and spirituality to an area that makes absolutely no money, that severely limits the amount of time that we can spend on it. Magickal teachers travel and have expenses. Research costs money. Time spent writing and putting together curriculums takes a lot of time and is worth something concrete in return.

The Christian lessons about simony have infected the way we transmit magick in the West, but it's important to recognize that even Christian churches need to fund themselves somehow. In non-congregational religions such as Wicca and Thelema, where everyone is ostensibly clergy, it's a bit harder to pass the plate around, so another method must be found. I have often suggested that Pagan priests who desire to do it full time might do well to model themselves on professional Houngans, Mambos, and Rootworkers, offering spiritual guidance for a small offering, but charging for magickal work.

The other issue with magick being treated as somehow *above* money is that very few genuine magicians would offer help to others. It can be a drain to help people with magick, but if there is some kind of concrete reward, it makes me much more willing to put in the time and effort. Lots of people volunteer for charities, but successful charities always seem to have a core of paid staff.

The charlatan argument is really just silly. Are there charlatans out there? Yes. They are unscrupulous people who take advantage of the throngs of people looking for magickal help. But if there weren't people out there looking for help, they wouldn't be able to scam them! Obviously there is a demand. Are you going to leave the supply up to the charlatans or are you going to allow genuine practitioners to step forward?

As I mentioned, many people seem to feel it's okay to charge for a tarot reading. Everywhere else in the world I have ever gone and gotten a reading, be it from an Italian strega or a Tibetan lama, I have been offered magickal assistance at the end of the reading. Most people seeking readers have a problem to solve, after all. Why offer them a reading that just lets them know what's in store and perhaps a few words of advice? Why not offer them a chance to change it with magick? Yes, if this is abused, it can fast turn into a scam, but it need not. Be truthful in your readings and offer reasonable options.

Reasons for Going Pro

Now that we have dealt with some of the taboos against doing magick for money, let's deal with some of the reasons in favor of it. The first and most obvious is money. Remember the section on financial wisdom and establishing secondary lines of income from something that you love and are passionate about? I assume that if you are reading this, you are probably passionate about magick. Some people give classes that they charge for. Some people create magickal tools that they sell. Doing magick for clients professionally is another way to gain income from something that you love.

In this day and age when New Age and occult stores are closing up left and right because of competition from the internet, a professional magick aspect to the shop can help bring in customers and compensate for that lost income. I helped a shop in Point Pleasant, New Jersey, set up candle altars shortly after they opened and they now have four different altars around the shop that people pay to have spells performed upon. Although other shops in the state are floundering, they remain open and thriving.

Money isn't the only reason to do magick for clients, though. There is also the practice. Some people treat practical magick as something that you do as a last resort. Unfortunately, it usually fails them at their most dire hour, because they don't have enough experience under their belts to make it work. It's just common sense. If you do something a lot, you get good at it. If you do it professionally, you will do it a lot. Ergo, you will advance in the art.

Charging for magick also helps get rid of frivolous requests. Often, if you are a Witch or magician, friends might bug you to do a spell for pretty petty things. It's a lark. Just as some people like to have a card reading done on a regular basis whether something is wrong or not, some people like to have magick done for them. Charging a reasonable sum for work done is something that will weed out those that are just out for kicks.

On the other side of that coin is the fact that people really in need of help will take you more seriously if you do charge. We live in a society that runs on money. It's that simple. If you give something away for free, most people will not attach value to it. If you charge for it, they will value it and respect it. I remember when I first started teaching classes in meditation. I taught them for free and a few people came and went, with no real consistency from class to class. When I moved the class to a New Age store in Philadelphia and started charging a fee, twice as many people showed up, and they came to every class consistently. I ask you: which was of benefit to more beings, doing it free or charging? To me, not only was I getting paid, but I was providing a better service to people who took it seriously.

Starting Out

If you want to do magick professionally, the first thing to do is, to put it bluntly, be sure you know your shit. Have a good grasp of the strategies in this book and a firm grounding in at least one magickal system. This is not an undertaking for just after you read this book. It should go without saying that you should be an adult. You should have been an adult for many years, in fact. You should have several years behind you of doing magick for yourself and your loved ones successfully.

How many years? It's hard to say. It depends upon the intensity of your work. Too many people calculate their experience in magick in terms of years instead of hours. I know people who have been "magicians" for twenty years, yet are completely incapable of dealing with even the slightest problem. Hanging out in occult stores, or paying for initiations in magickal orders, does not a competent Sorcerer make. On the other hand I have met people who have practiced intensely for as little as three years and are more than capable of handling themselves magically.

It's not necessary to get someone else's stamp of approval to be a successful Sorcerer. We are talking about practical magick here, not mysticism or spiritual guidance. If you can do it, you can do it. If you can't then you can't, no matter what degree you possess in the OTO or the local coven.

Deciding Your Level of Involvement

You can ruin any perfectly enjoyable and fulfilling hobby by turning it into a job. One of the real drawbacks to making money from doing something that you love is that you may find yourself doing a lot of things that you are not particularly interested in just to make a buck. You may even find yourself accepting work that you really do not want at all, just because you need the money. You need to decide right at the outset how deep you want to go.

I could pretty easily quit my day job and try to make it doing nothing but writing, teaching, and Sorcery. I don't though because I end up turning down many of the requests for Sorcery that I get. For instance, I never work on child custody cases. I don't usually perform break-up spells. I rarely will do curses, and never ones that aim to seriously injure a target unless they are known to be putting someone's life in danger. I also follow my instincts. If my inner guides are telling me not to take a client, I don't, even if it seems fairly harmless. If I depended upon magick as my primary income, I would be tempted to take on work that I know I shouldn't be doing.

You also need to think seriously about how clients contact you. I refuse to work from my phone, and limit my interactions with clients to email, so that I have a written record of everything. Most people however offer a phone number that they can be reached on. If you do offer a number, be sure clients know when they can and cannot call you. Be firm about it. If you let a client call you in the middle of the night, they will start calling all the time. I recently had to refuse a client who ended up getting my phone number from a store I teach at, just because she broke the rules of how to contact me. Whether you choose to do it as a secondary income or as your primary profession, you need barriers to keep your regular life separate from your job.

Expectations

You need to let people know what to expect when they hire you. People from countries and cultures where professional workers of magick are common tend to have more reasonable ideas of what to expect than people from mainstream American suburbia. Some will expect that a money spell will work almost instantly. Some literally will expect that money will just "show up" out of nowhere.

You need to be clear that magick works by manipulating probability, not by violating the laws of nature outright. Things happen, but they will take time and they will complement the efforts of the client. If your client is looking for financial help, there is nothing wrong with offering some of the financial advice that I gave in that chapter along with your spell. It's the same thing with finding love. If your client is a hopeless boob, you can of course do the spell for him, but it wouldn't hurt to offer him a plan to clean up and get some game in the process.

Under no circumstances should you *ever* guarantee success. Not only are you promising things that you possibly can't deliver, but you are opening yourself up to lawsuits and, in some states, arrest. Be clear that your clients are paying for traditional rituals and magick to be performed on their behalf; they are not paying for the exact result of those rituals. And, no, you don't offer a refund if the spell doesn't "work."

The situation is similar to that of a patient going to see a doctor. The doctor does his best to make a diagnosis and set forth a treatment. That is what you pay for: the examination and the medicine. He does not guarantee the medicine works, nor that his diagnosis is one hundred percent correct. If the cure doesn't work, it may require something stronger. It may require another examination by a specialist. In either case, the doctor does not issue a refund, because he has already invested his time and resources.

Keep in contact with your clients. Ask them what results they are getting. Some clients will not recognize that the extended over-time hours they just got asked to work are the results of the money spell they asked for. On the other hand, some clients will interpret almost anything as success. One client for whom I did a love spell was happy that he got a smile from a girl he liked and interpreted that as success. I insisted that it wasn't and went ahead and did a more powerful ritual for him to get a date with this girl. They have been dating for two years now. That is success.

There is no hard-and-fast rule for how long magick takes to work. Certain sympathetic magick spells work very fast, but offer fleeting results. Some spells that involve planetary intelligences take longer to work, but seem to lay the groundwork for long-term success better. My general rule though is that a spell should have at least a sign of working within three weeks, and should have a firm result within three months. Otherwise it's a failure.

Needless to say, we need to be respectful of probability. Rituals to get a job with a law firm will work only if you have gone to law school. You can engineer *probability* easily enough. Stretching the limits of *possibility* is a bit harder.

Methods

Before you can make a prescription, you will need to evaluate the client. Here is where your divination and intelligence gathering skills come into play. If you are a very skilled and detailed diviner, this might account for more than half the work you do, and you should charge appropriately whether you decide to do any additional work on the problem or not. On the other hand, if you charge primarily for spell work and do comparatively little divination on a case, you might offer the evaluation for free. That is what I generally do. I am only interested in getting a sense of the case and direction from my spiritual guides, not in providing the customer with a reading, so I don't charge. If the customer requests an online reading, that is another story. Once I get details from the client and a sense of the situation from my divinations, I can proceed.

Not everything that works well for you as a lifelong practitioner of magick will work well for a client whose only interest in magick is confined to the problem at hand. For instance, if you were experiencing psychic disturbances at night, you would probably do just fine with a banishing ritual performed every night for a few nights in a row. Your client however is not going to want to train in and perform a regular ritual or meditation unless the situation is really quite dire. You would be better off making him an amulet.

Keep in touch with the client and keep abreast of his or her progress. You can offer further assistance as things change, and it will be quite rewarding to know that your work has paid off. A year or so ago, I did a pro bono money spell for someone who wrote me in desperate need and was willing to send me pretty much their last dollar for help. I refused payment given their situation, but told the client that they could send me some money if and when the spell worked out for them. I never expected to hear from this person again.

Three months ago, I got an envelope at my post office box with a fifty-dollar check and a letter thanking me for my work. It seems shortly after my working, he finally found a job and was just starting to get some of his debt paid down. That felt really good.

NEW EDITION COMMENTARY—MORE THOUGHTS ON GOING PRO

A few years after I wrote this book, I quit my day job and started teaching and doing magick full time. I have not had a regular job in almost ten years. Devoting all my energies to my business became the key to success for me, but I did it only when I was absolutely certain I could support my family with what was coming in.

When I first started my company, Strategic Sorcery, I taught a course and offered readings and spellwork for hire. I also created large batches of talismans several times a year and put them up for sale. As time went on, I realized that I liked teaching courses way more than working with clients, so I started restricting my consultations to readings only. Eventually I dropped all one-on-one client work and all products that had to be physically shipped. As I was able to trim down what I did and focus on what I was best at and really loved to do, my business actually grew. Even more recently, I decided to stop teaching at conventions and festivals. Guess what happened? Yep, business grew again.

I am not sharing this with you because I think these are the universal keys to success, but to show that success will look different for everyone. You have to do more of what feeds you and gives you more energy to continue, even if that means letting some things drop. I have another friend that is almost the exact opposite of me. He feels energized and empowered by diving deep with individual clients and felt overwhelmed by offering online courses with many students, so he dropped the courses and focused on high-profile clients. He too wound up making more money by doing more of what he was great at and less of what he wasn't.

If you decide to become a professional Sorcerer, reader, teacher, or anything else related to magick, here are a few pieces of advice:

1. Avoid gimmicks. Magick is already something most of society looks at as either fake or evil, so do yourself a favor and play as straight as you can with people. Tell them what you are selling, why they might want it, and how much it is. Give them an easy way to pay you. That's it. You don't need to offer free e-books, worry about sales funnels, invest in SEO optimization, create false scarcity, or run a never-ending series of special deals. Do something useful. That's the secret. People buy

crappy products because of gimmicks all the time, but they never buy them *again*.

2. Figure out a price and stick with it: If you figured out what you want to make, and what you will offer people to make that, then stick with it. That is the cost. If you start offering special sales, that sale price becomes the new real price. People wait until the sale to buy, and those that don't get bitter about paying more than others. Drop out of the special sale prices and stick to your guns.

3. Profit must be your second concern. It needs to be a close second, but it must always be second. What comes first? Service. Service should lead all your decisions. When I need to make more money, I immediately ask myself, "How can I be of service to people in a way that would generate this income?"

4. Set firm boundaries and stick to them. There are a lot of unstable people out there, and unfortunately the Pagan and occult communities enjoy a larger-than-normal percentage. The more clients you serve and the more well-known you become, the more visible you will become. Your address, your day job, your phone number: these are all things that people can and will use and some will abuse. Those cute photos of your kids on Instagram stop being cute after your first stalker. Establish how you are comfortable being contacted and stick to it. Same thing with work hours.

PARTING WORDS

As I said in the introduction, this book is a field guide for practical Sorcery. Though there is certainly a lot of classical magick in the book, there is also a lot of information that isn't typically thought of as magick. I want my readers to stop thinking in terms of what is *magick* and what is not, and instead start thinking in terms of what is *successful* and what is not. The test of a Sorcerer is whether they can achieve success in their endeavors, which requires both skill at magick and skill in any other areas that can impact the situation. Skill in magick and ineptitude at life will not yield real results, only fantasies of power and wisdom.

Beyond this, the Sorcerer, Sorceress, or Sorcerix, as I see it, is a person who possesses not only occult knowledge, but also magickal power and mystical insight. Anyone can read spells out of a book and follow instructions. A genuine Sorcerer has accumulated internal power and wisdom, as well as spiritual allies. Through meditation, invocation, offerings, and energy work, the Sorcerer is able to know his or her true *will* and then live it with *skill*.

Although some magicians will perform magick only in sacred robes and consecrated circles, the Sorcerer takes magick to the street. He has the freedom to work within complex temples to perform ceremonies of evocation and to lay down sorcerous powders in his office or embed commands in his speech. By seamlessly blending temple magick and field magick with skillful living, he achieves his ends.

When it comes to spirituality, the Sorcerer acknowledges both the striving of matter to actualize itself within spirit, and spirit's inclination to manifest in matter. As such, there is no need to choose between practical magick and spiritual work, between Theurgy and Thaumaturgy. One is a reflection of the other. By mastering practical matters through Sorcery, we are freed to focus on illumination. By becoming illuminated, our Sorcery acts as the agent of spirit. Thus, the duty of the wise is fulfilled through the arcana of the hand and the eye.

IAO and the Greek Vowels

Throughout the book I use the word IAO as the primary invocation of divinity. Although the word has been interpreted in some places as a Greek form of YHVH, it really is much deeper than just that.

There are many ways to look at this most amazing word. The Golden Dawn, for instance, interpreted the word as an anagram of Isis, Apophis, and Osiris, signifying birth, destruction, and rebirth. This is useful within that system, but has much more universal meaning if we look back into history.

In Greek, of course, the vowels all relate to the planets, and this can be done either descending like this:

Alpha (A) = Saturn
Epsilon (E) = Jupiter
Eta (H) = Mars
Iota (I) = Sun
Omicron (O) = Venus
Upsilon (Y) = Mercury
Omega (W) = Moon

Or ascending like this:

Alpha (A) = Moon
Epsilon (E) = Mercury
Eta (H) = Venus
Iota (I) = Sun
Omicron (O) = Mars
Upsilon (Y) = Jupiter
Omega (W) = Saturn

In either case, IAO remains unchanged as the Solar syllable. Alpha and Omega alternate positions as the moon and Saturn = the beginning and end of the universe. So, by saying IAO, you are celebrating the sun as the Alpha et Omega.

Another interpretation is that you are literally reaffirming the self as "I" with the all.

There is, however, another more fundamental reason that the permutation IAO is primary and it has nothing to do with the planets. The chanting of vowels is an old Shamanic technique common the world over.

Slowly say IAO right now. Really drag each vowel out. The sound "I" is made by resonating sound in the *back* of the mouth near the soft palate. The "A" is generated in the *middle* of the mouth and is in Indio/Tibetan magick known as the "unfabricated sound," because there really is no manipulation of the mouth needed to utter it. The "O" is made at the lips and the *front* of the mouth near the teeth.

Say it again. The word literally travels from the rear to the front of your mouth. You are physically emanating the word from within to without, just as the universe was emanated from a singularity at the big bang. When said completely, all the other vowel sounds are present inherently, representing the entire ladder of lights.

APPENDIX 2

The Seven Seals

In the summer of 2007, I embarked on a project with my friend and longtime partner in crime Matthew Brownlee to generate a new group of planetary seals that would be able to access the sorcerous powers of the planets in a very direct and powerful manner. We wanted these seals not only to channel the forces of the powers invoked, but also to be able to overcome retrogrades, eclipses, and other unfortunate planetary alignments. In addition to this, we did not want them to be connected to any specific angels or deities, but to represent the planet in such a direct way that they could function well along side of Sumerian deities, Coptic archangels, Olympian gods, or with no religious or spiritual paradigm whatsoever.

Each seal is meant to represent the actual energetic pattern of the planet at work. The invocations were done by me, but the resulting vision that was to be the inspiration for the drawings was sent to Matt as the scryer. Through the combination of his own abilities and artistic talents, he was able to render a beautiful and effective set of seals. Each one recalls the classical astrological symbol that you are probably already familiar with, but weaves in the action of the planet.

In the original edition of this book there were only three of these planetary seals given: Venus, Mars, and Saturn. A few years later I produced a chapbook called *Advanced Planetary Magick* that gave all seven seals, forty-nine calls, and more info on the Greek vowels. The chapbook is still available on my website, but since this is the book where the seals were first introduced I thought it was appropriate to give all seven with a brief description of each.

Luna

When I first saw this seal, the manner in which the lines move across the crescent immediately called to mind the spooky way that passing clouds move over the moon. The next thing that drew me in was the spiraling at the center of the seal, calling to mind the powers of mind-bending illusion or possibly a descending spiral into lunacy. Looking closer at the spiral reveals it not to be a true spiral at the center but a crashing wave, calling to mind the moon's influence over the tides and waters.

The powers of Luna are many: deep intuition, illusions, time, love, dreams, sex, femininity, psychic powers, travel, water, and blood, just to name a few.

More than this, it is the moon that reflects the light of not only the sun, but the other planets as well. This reflective ability speaks to the nature of mind itself, which quite literally reflects the world around it based upon the sensory input it gets sent.

The moon, being closest to the earth, is also the gateway to the higher spheres and is thus an excellent astral body to work with when learning to astral project, scry, or develop any type of clairvoyance.

Real Sorcery

Mercury

Of all the seals we came up with, Mercury was the most elusive. Matt went through at least three different attempts before he could capture what was actually being revealed to him. Some were too jagged and lightning-like. Others were too fluid and lacked the speed and twistiness of Mercury. The visions that revealed the sigils showed patterns happening in more than three or four dimensions—this one was especially difficult to translate into two dimensions. The result was worth the effort, though. One of the first students who tested it wrote me saying that this seal was "like a high-powered technologically advanced microchip that makes the universe run more efficiently."

The powers of Mercury include thought, theft, intellect, business, marketing, movement, intelligence gathering, science, writing, games, and eloquence.

Venus

It was Matt who first pointed out that the arms of the sigil are reminiscent of a woman with one hand on her hair and the other on her hip. I can't say much more about it than that: the seal has the curves of a woman. There is also an element of ensorceling in the way that the line extending from the center circle wraps and writhes around the rest of the seal, almost like words that literally spellbind.

Venus, of course, rules emotions, love, friendships, romance, enchantment, beauty, art, parties, and pretty much all types of attraction and influence. It should also be noted that Venus is a force of generation. Without sex, there would be no life, and it was Haniel, the angel of Venus, that stories say the Lord sent to make the earth green.

Sol

This seal departs the furthest from the classic sigil that most people know. There is no circle with a dot on it. It does, however, have elements of the swastika in it and thus links to the rotation and spin of the sun. The sharp edges extending from it are reminiscent of solar flares. The right side of the seal is somewhat empty, which Sorath (a sun demon) tells me leaves "room for manifestation to occur." I feel it also speaks to the unpredictability and chaos at the heart of creation. In the center is a spiral of force emanating outward clockwise. This spiral also calls to mind the number six, which is the number of Sol.

The powers of the sun include ego, inspiration, true will, great gains, health, peace, youth, resurrection, promotions, and, if you are from Krypton, flight, super-strength, and heat vision.

Mars

This seal is an engine of martial power. When I first saw it, I immediately saw the center as a wheel of some immense war machine, or a reactor generating current. The force generated by the circle explodes outward in a sharp arrow-spike, as it does in the traditional sigil. In this seal, however, that force also releases out a looping lasso that draws whatever it snares inward towards the arrowhead.

The powers of Mars include war, conflict, defense, aggression, strength, competition, lust, courage, and confidence.

Real Sorcery

Jupiter

My favorite of the bunch. The origins of the classical seals is pretty obvious for most of them: the moon is a moon, Saturn is a sickle, etc. The classical Jupiter seal, however, looks to most people like a fancy four. It's not, though. It is derived from Jupiter's ever-present eagle. The body of the eagle is the vertical line, and the horizontal outcropping and bend are the wing. If you look at images of the Roman eagle, you will see it immediately.

Whereas the classic Roman eagle is perched and standing at attention, our seal is in flight. The curves and lines show how the winds support it and bring it what it needs.

The powers of Jupiter include grace, accretion, wealth, abundance, success, health, honors, materialism, and all that comes with it.

More than anything else, Jupiter is about sovereignty. Whether it be for money, or honors, or anything else, it is all for leading a life where you are the sovereign of yourself and your domain. It is for this element that the planet Jupiter is most often associated with the ruling deity of a pantheon: Zeus, Enlil, Dagda, Perun, Marduk, and of course Jehovah!

Saturn

The first thing to note about this seal is that the curved scythe of Saturn is on the opposite side from how it is in the traditional sign. Neither Matthew nor I are entirely sure why, but that is how it appeared, and it has been working well for people as it is. The second feature that I want to bring your attention to is the ribbon that entwines the entire seal. These are the ties that bind.

The powers of Saturn include death, binding, time, underworld, underground, darkness, decrease, the elderly, sleep, solitude, entropy, endings, and discipline.

Many people are afraid of working with Saturn, and it is indeed a heavy planet to work with, but whether we work with it or not, Saturn's influence will bear upon us. Better to know the path than walk it blind.

NOTES

Chapter 1

1. A caul is the amniotic sac that sometimes gets wrapped around the head of a newborn. Romany legend ascribes powers to those born with a caul. Certain Eastern European legends indicate that a child born with a caul may be a vampire. The caul was once a very sought-after charm against drowning. Charles Dickens's character David Copperfield tells of his parents auctioning off his birth caul for fifteen shillings.
2. Most people have a bit of royalty in their lineages somewhere along the line. For example, many genealogists believe that about eighty percent of English citizens can trace themselves back to Edward the Third.

Chapter 3

1. *Harvard Gazette,* April 18, 2002. Meditation changes temperatures: Mind controls body in extreme experiments by William J. Cromie.
2. *The Concealed Essence of the Hevajra Tantra with the Commentary Yogaratnamala* by G. W. Farrow and I. Menon.

3. Corrguineacht, or crane gesture, is performed on one foot, one eye closed, and one hand in belt. This was used by Lugh to incite the Men of Dea to battle against the Fomhoire.

Chapter 4

1. Asana is a type of position for meditation. Most famous is the lotus position, but the siddhasana, or half lotus, is much easier to do.
2. If you are going to study Abramelin, I recommend *The Book of Abramelin* translated and edited by Georg Dehn and Steven Guth.
3. Many thanks to Frater Xanthias for teaching me the invocation and providing me the translation.
4. Ngakpa literally means "mantra wielder" and is a type of Buddhist Tantric Sorcerer.

Chapter 5

1. She gained her psychic gifts after being hit on the head by a brick as a child.

Chapter 6

1. They are not as cool as James Bond, but they are probably the coolest comic book writer. All magick has its limits. . . .
2. If you didn't get the joke, then clearly you need to watch *Star Wars* again.
3. *Dbang gi phrin-las* in Tibetan.

Chapter 7

1. Fun fact: Father Karras in *The Exorcist* was played by actor and playwright Jason Miller.
2. According to a 2007 article in the *Eagle-Tribune* of North Andover, Massachusetts.
3. Name for Mercury.
4. In fact, you should think about it especially if you are in your twenties. I would kill to be able to go back in time and convince myself to set aside money when I was just out of school.

ABOUT THE AUTHOR

Jason Miller (Inominandum) has devoted thirty-five years to studying practical magick in its many forms. He is the author of six books, including the now classic *Protection and Reversal Magick* and *Consorting with Spirits*. He teaches several courses online including the Strategic Sorcery One-Year Course, the Sorcery of Hekate Training, and the Black School of Saint Cyprian.

He lives with his wife and children in the mountains of Vermont. Find out more at *www.strategicsorcery.net*.

ABOUT THE ILLUSTRATOR

Matthew Brownlee is an occultist, kung fu master, and tattoo artist located in Philadelphia, Pennsylvania. He is a member of the Chthonic Auranian Temple and is a Tantrika in the Nyingma and Bon lineages of Tibet. He is a graduate of the Philadelphia Art Institute and works as a tattoo artist in Rehoboth Beach, Delaware.

TO OUR READERS